SHADOWS
on Our
CATHOLIC "CHURCH"

Remaining as "Catholics" in
Spite of Our Church and the
Abuses by Our Clergy

A PASSAGE
With Brief History Points of Our Church

Rick Anthony Cordova

ISBN 979-8-88644-512-1 (Paperback)
ISBN 979-8-88644-516-9 (Hardcover)
ISBN 979-8-88644-513-8 (Digital)

Covenant Books
11661 Hwy 707
Murrells Inlet, SC 29576
www.covenantbooks.com

How many times have we pursued the seductive lights of power and celebrity, convinced that we are rendering good service to the Gospel!… How many times too, have we, as a Church, attempted to shine with our own light!

—Pope Francis
In his homily on the Solemnity of the Epiphany
January 6, 2019
(Vatican archive doc is dated January 13, 2018)

You are Peter, and upon this rock I will build my "church."
                                                        —*Matthew 16:18*

The "Church" of Jesus, the "Kingdom of God"

Is our Catholic "Church" a religious
"institution" centered on a bishop?

or

Is it a "way of life" focused and centered on God?

To *talk* of God is easy;

To *live* God requires authentic love.

Dedication

This book is dedicated to any member of our Catholic Church family who has experienced or endured personally, or witnessed others, being mistreated, dismissed, ignored, or abused in **any form** or **magnitude**, by a member(s) of our Catholic clergy and subsequently also by other members of our Church family through their inaction and overpiously keeping quiet.

It is also dedicated to any loving and authentic members of the clergy who sincerely show compassion and walk with victims and Christ; clergy who **live what they preach**.

Any form of abuse from within our church harms the **entire** Church. Any form of personal abuse inflicted by a member of our Church clergy will not necessarily be toward someone who is weak or naïve but will often be toward someone who has become trusting and vulnerable while living their faith into a deeper love of and for, **God**.

Love in any form such as kindness, unselfishness, compassion, etc. causes vulnerability through having our hearts wide open and trusting in the goodness of those around us, and through trusting in other's (often unauthentic) claim to or declaration of, their love for God, especially those within our Church who have **chosen** to be called "priests."

This book is also dedicated, humbly, to **"*parresia*"** and to being *"relentless" in our faith.* But above all, the intention of this book is dedicated to **God**.

Contents

Preface

Anyone can be a good and "holy" person, or a good "Christian" in any of countless religions, or even if part of no organized "religion" at all.

Jesus was a Jew.

Why is anyone a "Catholic"?

Why is anyone a "practicing" Catholic?

Ultimately, the only answers that are important are the ones between every "Catholic" and God and what is in each of our individual hearts.

Many Catholic diocesan clergy want laity to only know what they believe we "need" to know, and fear, feel threatened, or simply avoid, encouraging the faithful to get to know, question, understand, and embrace our religion and church institution with all of its human flaws. Perhaps it is fear of their clericalism being threatened and priesthood delegitimized. Even as simple as "What the heck is a 'Catholic'?" Lack of transparency is a **foolish reality** of our Church, for being authentic Catholics requires understanding what can be seen clearly in the warm light as well as what is obscured in the shadows of our church. It is in understanding our Church, both its ugly history as well as its beautiful history that one can come to love the **true** "Church" in spite of the failures of our "institution" of the Church which is human and often very disillusioning.

The issues discussed in this book do not even scratch the surface of how the Catholic Church deeply affects and harms members of its family. My story is only one of obviously countless experiences and accounts of many, all over the world, of **betrayal** by those in our church(s) who we are asked to trust, and who pretend or may even believe, to be following teachings of Christ.

How we got to where we are as a religion is intriguing; we should all as Catholics study any and whatever portions we can of the complicated formation and history of our Church. One can be drawn into a desire to learn more and more and into a deeper relationship and love with God through our faith in Jesus Christ. Our "Church," despite its institution, clergy abuses and failures, has survived by holding steadfast to that faith. Studying the framework of the Church, with or without support from clergy, and without fear of asking questions and of unpacking its shameful history and skeletons, one learns that there are over two thousand years of profound thought, meaning, purpose, and even beauty in Catholic theology, doctrine/catechism, canons, and basis, to what our Church **should** be teaching but **fails** horribly.

Our REAL and TRUE "Church," is obscured by the shadows and stains of our abusive clergy.

We can, however, continue to love our Catholic "Church" and to practice our "Catholic" religion as Christians, even if members of the clergy inflict harm, destroy their credibility as "priests," destroy desire and willingness of laity to participate in "their" churches, and whether or not victims can ever again come to trust those clergy and the very *human* institution of the Church.

Why does anyone who has personally experienced or witnessed others being harmed or deeply hurt or witnessed clerical abuses of any form or magnitude by member(s) of the clergy, who feels that he/she can no longer deal with the clericalism and seemingly lack of sincerity of priests, who feel forced to withdraw from the Church and avoid association with diocesan clergy, and who ultimately becomes a "victim" of the Church remain a "Catholic"?

I like to believe it is as simple as the "victim" keeping in mind that any member of the clergy is only a single human member of the Church himself, and that any abusive member of the clergy who does not <u>aspire</u> to authentically live a holy, loving, and humble life is not living a life that follows Church theology, doctrine, canons, or more importantly, the mission of Christ. Unfortunately, priests never act alone but with support from their fraternal brothers as well as from overpious laity and clericalism, lack of accountability, and their collars protect them. But <u>**we**</u> can be true, authentic, loving Catholic Christians, even if some of our clergy might not be.

This book is based on public information available as well as the personal opinion and accounts of one member of the Catholic Church, RAC, who has been deeply harmed as an active participating Catholic through personally witnessing various magnitudes and forms of abusive (nonsexual), elitist, and unkind behavior *repeatedly* by members of diocesan clergy, who thrive on their clericalism/elitism and turn their backs on those they hurt with a callus lack of remorse while those in the pews overpiously don't understand or care of the harm done, just keep quiet (sometimes in denial), or simply stop attending church altogether, hurt or even angry. All of us at some time or other wonder how anyone can allow "priests" to abuse the gift of their priesthood, or for oneself to be abused. **All** Catholics are indoctrinated to believe "priests" are holy and "special." **All** Catholics allow clericalism and clerical abuse of some form and level of magnitude by "men" who happen to be "priests" (?) and whose moral integrity is <u>trusted</u>.

It is said that the opposite of love is <u>not</u> hate, but rather INDIFFERENCE **and not caring.** Our Church is infested with indifference and self-interest by our diocesan clergy. We, as "Christian" laity, though, should all care about how all our family members, <u>not only immediate family</u>, are respected, treated, and loved in our church communities, especially by our clergy.

To victims, I offer support of many (even of those who with weakness or fear choose to keep silent) and pray that the flames in the hearts of victims may continue to shine or be rekindled to shine, in spite of abusive, hurtful members of the clergy and that they may remain open to meeting and getting to know other members of our Church clergy, who **do** exist <u>somewhere</u> within one of the many orders in our Church, living authentic, "spiritual" vocations.

To laity whose discipleships are <u>interrupted</u> by the shadows cast by abusive clergy and blinded and misled toward a distorted cause of God by their clericalism and elitism, I pray that they may <u>never</u> be afraid of, nor intimidated or impressed, by any member of our clergy simply for wearing a collar, or by their clericalism, and that they may be inspired by other members of the clergy with true vocations striving to live examples of lives dedicated to the <u>true</u> cause of God.

To those members of the clergy who apathetically and with such indifference hurt, mislead, and drive laity from their churches or from actively practicing as Catholics, I pray that their hearts be softened; that they come to the realization and remorse for the harm they inflict and for their false claims of service to the cause of God, that they come to know the God they preach of, for true formation of hearts in our Catholic seminaries, and for reform within the Catholic Church.

To those authentic members of the Catholic clergy who are proactively part of God's mission moving forward (and if humble, do not even know they are), I sincerely thank them and pray that they continue to strive to be humble examples of true disciples of Christ, regardless of contrary clergy to whom they are obligated to be fraternal and who they could potentially (hopefully) maybe one day inspire. May God continue to abundantly bless them.

I pray for humbleness in each of us as "Christians," that every member of the Catholic clergy, and each of us, whether a member of the Catholic Church or not, will never be afraid to look inward and question our own authenticity when we "claim" to be "disciples" and "followers of the teachings of Christ." May our church regain focus and sight on God rather than in its belief and obsession in its own false sense of "godliness."

Prologue

A *shadow* is defined as a dark figure that is cast on a surface by a body intercepting or blocking the rays from a light source. Within our Church, a *shadow* can also be the darkness cast by anyone who believes he is a source of light to bring attention to oneself.

Abusive behavior(s) by Catholic priests cast shadows on our churches, not by intercepting or blocking the light of the Holy Spirit, which is not possible, but **by blocking the perception and the attention of the laity to that "Light,"** including **when priests believe and attempt to give impression that they themselves are a source of the "light."** Priests who abuse their positions and religious authority interrupt and deflect the <u>reception</u> of the light of the Holy Spirit and leave their shadows as stains on our churches and in the hearts of those who pray there.

Discussion on "abusive" behavior of priests is usually focused on sexual abuses; but abuse may be physical, emotional, spiritual, financial, clericalism, abuse of clerical position and authority, elitism, false sense of exaltation, or simply by intentionally turning their backs on someone.

Call it sexual or physical abuse; call it intimidation by clergy; call it clericalism; call it abuse of their clerical position; call it taking advantage of fundraisers, donations, meals, and exploiting the piety and generosity of parishioners and donors; call it opportunistic excessive travel; call it elitism and maintaining separation between the clergy and the laity; call it unnecessary expenditures on excessive and overextravagant vestments; call it turning their back on someone who reaches out to them for help.

"ABUSE" is "ABUSE."

No matter what we call it or its level of
magnitude, fostered by clericalism.

Abuse is also another priest who witnesses or is made aware of the abuse and makes light of it or keeps silent, aggravating the harm inflicted, including if it is for fear of fraternal conflict.

Abuse by clergy begins in what may seem small insignificant acts and becomes more and more prevalent, harmful, and damaging as comfort, self-interest, arrogance, narcissism, callousness, and lack of remorse and accountability progresses; and the faithful keep quiet.

In August of 2018, Pope Francis wrote a "Letter to the People of God" in response to the report the Church had just released regarding more than a thousand victims of sex abuse by clergy. In the letter, Francis acknowledged how *the wounds never go away" and the "heart wrenching pain…and cries had been long ignored, kept quiet, or silenced."*

Five years earlier in 2013, Francis had been passed the torch from Pope Benedict who inherited heavy abuse issues and, overwhelmed, resigned as pope (without an apology). When a pope renounces and relinquishes his position as "pope," it is an event of major consequence in our Church, including to validate the human fallibility of the pope. It was striking that in the Letter to the People of God, Francis wrote, *"I make my own the words of the then Cardinal Ratzinger,"* quoting Ratzinger **prior** to becoming "Pope Benedict":

> *How much filth there is the Church, and even among those who, in the priesthood, ought to belong entirely to [Christ]! How much pride, how much self-complacency! Christ's betrayal by his disciples, their unworthy reception of his body and blood, is certainly the greatest suffering endured by the Redeemer; it pierces his heart. We can only call to him from the depths of our hearts: Kyrie eleison Lord, save us! (cf. Mt 8:25)* (Cardinal Ratzinger in 2005)

The following month after his letter to the people of God, in September of 2018, Pope Francis acknowledged, *"There is something I have understood with great clarity…abuse…has behind it a Church that is elitist and clericalist, an inability to be near to the people of God."* Francis very clearly has recognized that **"Elitism, clericalism fosters every form of abuse"** (Pope Francis to Jesuits in 2018).

The sad reality is that **if** and after hands are slapped, abusive priests continue to have a welcome even exalted place in the church while their victims, those they vowed to serve, remain abandoned in a painful struggle whether they remain in the Church, are driven away from the church they love, or in extreme cases, are driven even to commit suicide.

The elitism and clericalism by clergy and the various forms of abuse it fosters, as Francis warned about several years ago, continue blatantly by US clergy who cover for each other. No one can teach or force our clergy to strive for humbleness and holiness, or to surrender their lives to God, even through the vows they take at their ordination. **That can come only from one's heart.**

The reader should keep *"Parresia"* (see pages 36 and 122) in mind throughout this entire book. **This book is not intended to criticize our "church" or to be cynical, but to support victims, raise questions, and bring to discussion the failings of our very <u>human</u> Church <u>institution</u>**, which affects all Catholics, which was built by <u>**fallible men**</u> in God's name, which is led and guided by <u>**fallible**</u> bishops and church leaders, and which is not always in accordance to the **teachings of Christ.**

How do victims of any mistreatment or abuses through clergy self-interest continue within the Catholic Church they love?

How does one continue as a "Catholic" when clergy destroy their own credibility as "priests" to you and cause you to need to completely withdraw and avoid them?

How do <u>harmed</u> members of the faithful continue to practice their religion of choice "without" their <u>local</u> priest(s) or physical church(s)?

Answers to these questions can also only be discovered between each "victim" and God. But some facts are held certain by <u>ALL</u> people of true faith: God the Father, Son, and the Holy Spirit, as Jesus very physically showed His disciples, cannot be kept out by locked doors, closed hearts, or self-consumed actions by past and <u>present-day </u>Pharisees and "high" priests.

It is **NOT** academia or graduation from a seminary, but rather <u>humbleness and love</u>, with which one comes to know God and the teachings of Jesus. Regardless of training or education in seminaries and theological universities or the expertise in man-made doctrines and Canon Laws, no human being can ever be an "expert" on "God" nor on another individual's relationship with God, and no human being can ever pretend to know what God's will is other than the accounts of His Word in scripture and His greatest commandment: for us to love and live in His love.

The depth and meanings in scripture are profound and limitless. This can be seen even as simply as in how different clergy will, at times even sadly, personally interpret and reflect on the Gospels in their weekly homilies. Every time we read scripture, we open ourselves to be enlightened into a <u>deeper</u> understanding and a <u>deeper</u> enlightenment. The "Word" is a "living" gift from God to mankind. The principal language in the Roman Empire was Greek and the original books in the Bible were written by men in Greek and some Aramaic. There are many who claim that since authors were Jews, that much was written in Hebrew and Aramaic. What is important, though, is that sometimes, the full depth in sentiment and meanings are lost in translations, especially into the English language. All languages have words and expressions that have no direct translation. Pope Francis, who is known to be most fluent and comfortable with Italian, Spanish, and Latin languages, speaks and writes incredible, beautiful letters, messages, and homilies; but the mere translation into English often takes away from the depth of his messages which without question come from his heart.

*"**Peace** I leave you, My **Peace** I give to you.
<u>Not as this world gives</u> do I give it to you. Do not let
your hearts be troubled or afraid"* (Mark 14:27).

The word *peace*, as a very simple example, is a word said to be used in the Bible approximately four hundred times. The word *peace* is also said to have <u>not even appeared</u> in the English language until the twelfth to thirteenth centuries and derived from French *paiz*, Latin *pacisci*, Spanish *paz*, Italian *pace*. Would Jesus have used a shallow word *peace* when there is a beautiful, more profound **Hebrew** word, *"Shalom?"*

"Shalom" is used to both greet people and to bid them farewell. **Shalom** is more than just simply peace; it is a complete peace. It is a feeling of contentment, completeness, wholeness, well-being, and harmony. **Shalom** means health, peace, welfare, safety, soundness, tranquility, prosperity, perfectness, fullness, rest, harmony, the absence of agitation or discord. **Shalom,** from the root verb *shalam* means perfection, to be complete and full. The word *shalom* is spoken as a powerful and profound blessing. *"Death and life are in the power of the tongue"* (Prov. 18:21). So when we greet and bless someone with the word *shalom*, we are wishing and blessing into their life all the wonderful and profound graces and wishes from a deep and warm place in our heart, with all that *"shalom"* implies. Who knows what God's "word" would have been or how He would have expressed it, but Jesus gives us something much deeper and beyond just "peace" which clergy within the Institution of our Church have <u>NO</u> control over any of us.

"Peace ^{Shalom} *I leave you, My Peace* ^{Shalom} *I give to you. **Not** as this world gives do I give it to you"* (Mark 14:27).

The <u>acts, words, and teachings of Jesus</u> are so profound that how can we possibly even imagine, fathom, or pretend to fully capture the depth of His Word in written accounts and translations by <u>human men</u> about Jesus, but most importantly with our **human limitations of love and speech**.

As Catholics, we trust in the *"magisterium"* of our Catholic Church, the authority of the Church to <u>authentically</u> not only to <u>interpret</u> what was written and what was by "tradition" handed down through generations of word of mouth, but to also <u>teach</u> the Word of God. Derived from the Latin term *magister*, meaning "teacher," the intention of *"magisterium"* is not solely that the Word be properly interpreted and preached, but that it also be <u>properly put into action through example</u>.

God does not and would <u>never</u> exclusively enlighten only Catholic clergy. **TRUTH is TRUTH**, regardless of its interpretation and regardless of the relativism by which right-wing clergy protect their clericalism and elitism and resist Vatican II, as definitely seen in the United States.

When we make ourselves present, the Holy Spirit guides each and every one of us individually into deeper understanding, and the Holy Spirit even guides each and every one of us in whether to trust the authenticity and credibility of our clergy as "priests." Every one of them is human, and as it has been proven throughout the history of our Church, every single member of the clergy is fallible and every part of the human <u>institution</u> of our Church has the potential to be modified and reformed so that **the cause of God** is truly administered. We are <u>all</u> the "Church."

Our Catholic Church is blessed to be led by our current pope in whom many of us trust and find credibility toward Church "magisterium." What Pope Francis very publicly and transparently asks of both clergy and laity reflects his belief in Jesus Christ, the theology of the Church and the cause of God. He very obviously believes in and is committed to Vatican II and what it means to be "Catholic." The <u>failure</u> and <u>lack of accountability</u> of clergy to support and respond to directives of Pope Francis aggravates the loss of credibility of clergy through all forms of abuse.

The "Denunciation [by Jesus] of the Scribes and Pharisees" is a lengthy chapter (23) in the gospel of Matthew against clericalism, hypocrisy, and self-indulgence. In his abidance to the teachings of Jesus throughout his papacy, Pope Francis has <u>repeatedly</u> denounced clericalism, elitism, and clerical abuses within the hierarchy of the Church. So is that systemic clericalist nature in our Church and the defiance by clergy to the directives and countless messages by Pope Francis, the result of sheer disobedience of the pope by Catholic bishops and clergy? Or is the message and "mission" of the teachings of Jesus throughout scriptures simply **not** accepted and understood down through the ranks of the Institution of our Church?

It is said that each and every one of us has an incredible influence on others, which is immortal. Can any **one** of us even **imagine** what the impact of Catholic influence would be if our bishops and priests within every church of every diocese, inspired the members of their parish "families" with loving humbleness and authenticity rather than with arrogance, self-indulgence, and self-interest and indifference?

How can the lives of our "priests" be examples of loving humbleness and authenticity if blatantly lived with the false sense of royalty and the claim that "holiness" and the requirement for their exaltation comes "<u>automatically</u>" with priestly ordination?

How can clericalism, clerical abuses, and self-indulgence even coexist with true humbleness and love for God in their hearts? I believe <u>it cannot</u>.

How did the apostles, <u>living alongside Jesus</u>, live <u>their</u> lives as "<u>examples</u>"?

The apostles were uneducated; religiously and socially unrefined men; men of short tempers, selfishness, jealousy, greed, and ambition. Only one of the apostles understood the power of the ministry and teachings of Jesus even perhaps to the extent of disillusionment from hope in Jesus leading an army against the Romans, and it was he who first betrayed Jesus. In the beautiful *"Prayer of Jesus"* before he was arrested, Jesus refers to him as having lost only one of His apostles, *"the son of destruction, <u>in order that the scripture might be fulfilled</u>"* (John 17:12). Judas understood Jesus as the "Messiah," but he did not hold to his own belief and faith in Jesus, and seemingly destroyed the saving power of his own deep remorse through his misdirected focus, despair, and suicide. How would history have changed had Judas, truly remorseful, not fallen to suicide? The remaining apostles did not comprehend most of what Jesus explained to them nor the actions and miracles that He performed right in front of their eyes. In the Gospel of Mark, we see Jesus display deep frustration: *"Do you not yet understand or comprehend? Are your hearts hardened? Do you* *have eyes and not see; ears and not hear? And do you not remember?"* *(Mark 8:17–18).*

Jesus continues repeating these questions to each member of our clergy and to all "Christians."

From scripture, we also know that the apostles were not always kind to those who tried to get near to or to be around Jesus. Much in the same way as to preventing outsiders from becoming part of their "clique" with Jesus, or even to the point of complete exclusion. On occasion, they would try to convince Jesus to ignore those who were not Jews or Gentiles such as Samarians, Canaanites, etc.; to "dismiss" those who were reaching out for Jesus and following Him as "they" walked. Even children…it takes a hardened heart to *"rebuke"* children and push them away from anyone, especially from Jesus (Mark 10:13–16).

So we can't even pretend to imagine how painful it must have been for Jesus, even while always knowing that His apostles were weak and would betray and abandon Him during His arrest, trial, and crucifixion and continue to betray Him to this day.

It is thought-provoking to think that the Pharisees and high priests, who were already determined to have Jesus crucified, had been scheming behind the scenes on the timing of the arrest of Jesus because of Passover and their fear of how the people would react, *"for they were afraid of the people" (Luke 22:2)*; afraid of a *"riot among the people" (Matt. 26:5)*. While the apostles in turn, were afraid to stand with Jesus.

Only one of the apostles, however, *"the one Jesus loved,"* who knew and believed in Jesus, stood at the foot of the cross with His soul-wrenched mother Mary, available for Jesus to entrust her into his home and care. The other apostles were either hiding in fear or running in despair.

Just like the original apostles, the Pharisees, and high priests, our Catholic clergy are only men, and <u>nothing more than men</u>, who happen to be "priests."

Just like that of the original apostles, the lives of our priests do not change, and their ministries do not fully commence until and after each of their individual "Pentecosts," when the Holy Spirit is thrust upon them and is welcomed to embrace their heart in their love for God, whenever that might occur in each of their individual lives (or not).

Just prior to walking to His sleeping apostles and be arrested, Jesus prayed to His Father, *"I will make it known that the love with which You loved me may be in them and I in them"* (John 17:26).

When priesthood is entered into with devotion and sincerity, it is one of the most admirable of human "professions," but <u>when the GIFT of priesthood is abused</u>, it can be perhaps the ugliest of all human professions, consumed in self-interest with arrogance and hypocrisy, and with little or no accountability or even remorse.

It is important, though, to stress that <u>many</u> priests <u>DO</u> sincerely dedicate their lives to God and <u>DO</u> sincerely strive to inspire others to live holy lives <u>by their loving example</u>.

Many others unfortunately, inflict harm, through self-interest, pride and personal ambition(s), interfering with the love that laity often prefer to believe might just be hidden or trapped in their hearts. Others, obviously simply don't comprehend, just as the original apostles did not, whether they enter the seminary as educated, religiously and socially refined men, **or not**.

Priesthood has many human traps, which takes true spirituality, faith, and sincere desire, devotion and love to overcome. Anyone can put on a collar, wear extravagant vestments, gaudy excessive capes, memorize doctrine and be taught to read the Gospel. It takes an <u>authentically</u> <u>humble</u> heart directed to God, to be a true "priest."

Only an insecure man, wearing a "priest" collar, arrogantly blinded by his own false "light," craves the personal ambitions, the rise in the hierarchy and title, to <u>demand</u> respect, rather than the respect attained from admiration of a humble example, authentic love for God, and a vocation to the cause of God which he <u>receives</u> <u>and</u> **<u>considers</u>** <u>to be</u> **<u>solely</u>** a **gift and blessing** from God.

That of a true *VOCATION*...

> *VOCATION*...*is not*...*a goal to be achieved*...
> *but a **GIFT** to be received.*
> *VOCATION does not come from <u>a voice "out
> there"</u> calling me **to become** <u>something I am not</u>.*
> *It comes from <u>a voice "in there"</u> calling me **to
> be** <u>the person I was born to be</u>, to fulfill the original SELFHOOD given me at birth by **God**.* (Parker Palmer)

"Follow me."

We Begin This Book with Prayer

He was praying in a certain place, and when he had finished, one of his disciples said to him *"Lord, teach us to pray."* (Luke 11:1–2)

Jesus said: *When you pray, do not be like the hypocrites, who love to stand and pray in the synagogues and on street corners so that others may see them. Amen I say to you, they have received their reward in full. But when you pray, go to your inner room, close the door and pray to your Father in secret. And your Father, who sees what is done in secret, will reward you. And when you pray, do not keep on babbling like pagans, for they think they will be heard because of their many words. Do not be like them, for your Father knows what you need before you ask him.* "This, then, is how you should pray":

> **Our Father in heaven,**
> **hallowed be your name,**
> **Your kingdom come,**
> **Your will be done,**
> **on earth as it is in heaven.**

Give us today our daily bread.
And forgive us our debts,
as we forgive our debtors.
And lead us not into temptation,
but deliver us from the evil one. (Matt. 6:5–13)

Amen.

HEAVENLY FATHER

Whatever religion we practice on our walk with You,

Help us to remember where we came from,

Who our source of life is,

Whose breath is in our body, and

Who has cradled and kissed our souls and knows us perfectly.

Help us understand and embrace why we are here;

On our own Road to "Galilee" even if we take detours to our "Emmaus";

Here to answer Your call to discipleship,

To remember what you taught us through Your human life,

and to have our hearts fully open to You;

Help us always to keep in mind where we are going;

Back to You, with You, as a part of You and You in us,

To be with You always, in Your Presence

To be in and part of Your love

In the name of the Father, the Son, and the Holy Spirit,
Amen.

Foreword

In the summer of 2012, a "diocesan" priest, the rector of the cathedral of the diocese of El Paso, Texas, passed away unexpectedly while visiting Chicago. He, like all priests, was no more than a man who happened to be a priest. He was a good man, respected, admired, and loved by many. Perhaps what made him special and "different" as a priest was that he was not trained, indoctrinated, or mentored as a "diocesan" priest. He had incardinated into the diocesan order of priesthood from the Society of Mary (Marist) for reasons maybe only he knew deep within himself, and only he knew if he ever regretted.

Marists are a religious order devoted to Mary. According to the Marists, they believe Mary was the first disciple of Jesus and the mother of the Church. Marists also believe that the power given to a Christian by the Holy Spirit is characterized by *"mercy and compassion, availability, welcome and hospitality, simplicity manifest in everyday ordinariness and a common touch…that they are self-effacing apostles who demonstrate a spirit of joy and respect for others; <u>called to be humble and hidden and unknown in the world</u>"* (Marist US Province Identity Statement).

One would think that those Marist beliefs would be also those of <u>any</u> order of clergy, but nevertheless, they obviously were a strong foundation for the life our rector tried to share through his ministry.

Religious order clergy follow the rules and lifestyle of the institution they are part of, and take vows of poverty, chastity, and obedience. Diocesan priests do not take vows of poverty and promise to be obedient to the bishop of the diocese they belong to. In recent ordinations, after our candidates take their vows they are asked to come up the altar stairs to stand at eye level with our seated bishop, where he firmly grips their hands and with "laser" eye contact asks them, *"Do you PROMISE to be obedient and respectful to **ME** and my successors?"* They renew their "promises" every year at the Chrism Mass, which ironically is celebrated during Lent, a season for opening hearts, looking inward, and of atonement. In reality, though, with so much lack of accountability and transparency, and according to Canon Law, once the bishop assigns the parish priest, the pastor is in charge of the parish and the bishop does not have much to say, do, or to pretend to dictate or enforce other than general policies of the diocese, or to remove/move him depending on their initial agreement. True discipleship requires commitment and strength. For diocesan priests, clericalism, elitism, and abuse of clerical position is common; self-interest and human weaknesses make it an almost impossible challenge not to seek and enjoy the limelight, being considered a celebrity, being revered, wined and dined, and to enjoying a more than just comfortable lifestyles. Laity exacerbate the problem. Some diocesan priests, comfortable with their way of life, have justified this by admitting that they did not take a vow of poverty.

For most of the faithful who met or got to know this "once religious order priest" during his fifteen years as rector of the cathedral, it came easy for each of them to believe in their hearts that they were his best friend, but most importantly, everyone <u>knew</u> that he truly cared. Those who listened to him were inspired, not only spiritually to deepen their relationship with God, but also religiously to get to know and understand their religion better. He would advise, if one sees something wrong in our Church, not to leave it…but rather to help to fix it. A tall order from someone familiar with the inside workings of the church behind the scenes, that require personal strength of character and commitment to true discipleship. For reaching out to and within the fraternity of diocesan priests can be like pushing a rope if one challenges something clergy are comfortable with and don't want to change. To overcome difficulties, his charge to the community was always and passionately to *"be relentless!"* While he was around, though, no one in the community ever really ever seemed to have much religious reason to be unhappy with or to pay much attention to wrongs of "our" Church. Unlike our diocesan clergy, he was never <u>afraid</u> or <u>too busy</u> to listen, even if to only try to understand another viewpoint. Where one least expected, he could find a source of grace. With open arms, all were welcome and invited to get involved and to participate including at Sunday Mass where they would come from every parish and nearby cities even though he would avoid publicly disclosing, which mass(s) he would be presiding at. He was blunt in saying that if anyone was coming to mass because of him they were coming for the wrong reason. But every single member of the faithful who tried to celebrate mass with him knew, as does every "victim" who has experienced or witnessed abusive behavior by clergy knows, that it does in fact, very much so, make a difference that the authenticity of a priest's devotion to God, both on and off the altar, **be credible**.

As his imploding "life" within the community progressed, he could no longer go to a restaurant, go shopping for basic necessities, relax in public, or even visit the doctor and get medical attention, without someone recognizing him, knowing him, wanting his attention, or interrupting and invading his personal privacy. To have a place to quietly get away, he tried to keep having a private condo, a secret. His ministry and becoming "diocesan" came with a double-edged sword. Before he knew it, becoming widely known and popular was out of control. The laity was drawn to him like rock star groupies, and many were unfamiliar with the quality of pastoral care the likes of his that is almost always lacking in diocesan priests, so they, from every parish, were drawn to him. It made his ministry as an example, appropriate for the cathedral of any diocese of any city. A failing on his part, though, was seemingly coming to believe, as he quietly stated that to be a good priest, one had to be a good actor. He was lauded by some and criticized by others for becoming a little theatrical at times just so as to reach those that might require a little drama to come to church.

But a true and humble priest might not let on what he may personally be experiencing on any given day or period in his life. He might preside at the funeral of a dear friend while on the same day also preside at the wedding or the joyful celebration of another. He might be having a bad day or not feeling well and thinks he needs to keep that from showing as he walks into a meeting or steps onto the altar sanctuary. Many a "priest" may simply attempt to pretend to be holier than what he really is. Being always publicly forthright and transparent, though, is what helps anyone to be authentic, to be at peace with oneself, and to be a reflection and example of that to others. If not diligent and careful, one begins to have to wear two faces, and the life he lives off the altar and behind the scenes become different from what he preaches at the ambo.

Our rector's homilies were always rooted in his heart, and as far as most of us ever witnessed, his credibility as a priest was never questioned, compromised, or lost. Against his choosing, though, he had fallen into and knew not how to avoid or deal with the trap that lays in front of all priests, definitely diocesan priests, and which he worked hard to avoid: that of being treated as a celebrity priest, and to being raised up onto a pedestal. So in what I can only imagine must have been a painful and extremely lonely passage...he was in Chicago with a friend whom he trusted and allowed him to be himself—intending to be away, to get away, 1,500 miles away, for only a few days, and subsequently died physically, mentally, and spiritually in a condition and manner no one ever should, away from his home and away from his church "family" who loved him...perhaps too much, or perhaps in the wrong way...because he had become a *celebrity* "priest" being suffocated by so many reaching out to him and who very much loved him.

But those who had been truly open and fully attentive to his ministry were inspired and challenged into a deeper place in their faith and into a deeper place in their discernment of their personal individual journey(s). But perhaps also, they just possibly may have been directed onto a path to be a continuation of the mission that God had created him for and which he may or not have been able to complete. Only God knows. Trying to do his "job" did not make him a saint, but one thing is certain, though: his was a special ministry and discipleship...cut short. With him, died a true ministry at our cathedral and within the entire church. He was fifty-seven years young.

Twenty years earlier, my mom at a family gathering had choked and fallen into what would turn out to be a permanent coma of several years. Not until many years later, while going through some papers, would I learn that my dad, not long before this, had a minor stroke. My mom and dad were the greatest examples of love and altruistic lives my two brothers and I have ever known. Growing up, my brothers and I were inseparable; their love has been an example to me throughout my life of God's love. After being removed from the respirator and out of ICU into her hospital room, a member of the family was always with her; my dad would stay the night. She was constantly tended to in as dignified a manner as possible and in personal sleeping gowns cut and hemmed in the back and laundered at home. Prayer and constant love kept hope alive that she would suddenly "wake up." For the first year, my maternal grandmother's trek to the hospital was a daily sacrifice. As her carotid artery, heart, and personal struggle deteriorated, she passed away the day before New Year's eve down the hall, a few rooms away from my mom's.

I was an officer of our university student engineering chapter, and faculty and peers convinced me to attend an installation held in the outskirts of the city. On the way home, through a dark, desolate section of the desert highway, we were in a horrific accident involving a death, which everyone in the car had thought was a large animal, and which would change our lives. It was a homeless woman with no identification. Wearing several layers of clothes and with only a couple of coins in her pocket, the closest that investigators could determine the age of her badly neglected body was between twenty and forty years old. With no understanding of why someone in that condition would be roaming the desolate highway in the dark and would run in front of a vehicle from the highway median, they figured she was deranged or had committed suicide. But this human being we had never met would become a profound part of the rest of our lives. After hours of investigation out in the dark desert highway late that night, I somehow got myself to the hospital to talk to my dad before any TV news broadcast. By the time I reached the door to my mom's hospital room and turned to look behind me, three nurses, who had come to know our family, were reaching to me concerned apparently of the shock I was carrying on my face. I don't know why God would allow another tragic trauma during that period in our lives, but one thing is certain to me: that one of the many detectives involved was more of a "priest" than almost anyone I've ever met who wears a Catholic collar.

To this day, I've remained grateful and kept him and his family in my prayers. True loving human beings very personally feel and fully absorb the pain of others as if their own and walk with them. They have an extremely powerful strength of character to be of selfless service to others, just as we've seen in medical caregivers who have never hidden from fear or from shear inconvenience, to help others during the COVID pandemic, something we don't see in most of our diocesan clergy. Indifference and elevated self-worth keeps that strength of character from developing within the majority of Catholic diocesan clergy while one by one, Catholics stop attending and participating at church.

Our family "life" going back and forth to the hospital continued, and about a year and half later, we moved my mom to be cared for at home rather than to a nursing facility. After a clouded way of life at home with full-time nursing, she was rushed to the hospital and passed away in our arms and God's embrace. Ironically, like our rector, she also was fifty-seven years young. Throughout those extremely painful years, our stoic grandfather had never been the same again, and his own health slowly deteriorated and my dad's heart issues continued. For several years, my dad would help bathe him, help him retain some continued dignity and purpose in life, and prepare dinner for him and everyone else who would continue to visit every Sunday until his ninety-eight-year-old body surrendered. During those difficult years, several close friends and several very close and loved paternal uncles and aunts also passed away, one in a horrible accident, others through cancer or heart conditions. With everything that had been going on, I had delayed my university plans and graduation. I passed on professional opportunities. My relationships were affected, especially with a wonderful girl whom I will always care for and hold in a special place in my heart.

Then, when we least expected, my dad was diagnosed with esophageal cancer. After a valiant fight, remission, reoccurrence, and hospitalization with complications at Houston MD Anderson, the doctor, knowing the end was near, in a sincere and loving way, asked for our permission to ask our dad the horrible "question": if he would prefer to die at home. My dad never hesitated to answer in a very peaceful, faith-filled manner. The doctor then asked if we would allow him to pray. He prayed for my dad, for God's guidance to the doctors and medical staff, and for us his sons, in a very spiritual and touching way—one which we had never thought was possible or ever witnessed by a doctor. His sweet nurse struggled, having to leave my dad's room holding back tears and, with her loving heart overwhelmed, apologized as she embraced us. A few hours later, the doctor performed a tracheotomy to make the trip home possible, and with my brothers and sister-in-law, in a small ambulance plane, we transferred my dad back to El Paso. After a few weeks in a local LTAC that was walking distance from his home, a few days after his birthday, in the early hours of the morning, a few hours after my brother and I let him know we were taking him home, he passed away. My brother and I had left only to prepare his room at home for the medical equipment we would be receiving the next day, when the phone call came. We rushed back, but as we entered my dad's room, he was already cradled in God's embrace. As we bowed down on his still warm chest and hugged him one final time, the last breath my dad had taken before he died was expelled with a sound of a "wind" and a relief from his lungs as if to sending a profound message to us and bestowing on us his blessing.

After many years as caregivers and back-to-back deaths in our lives, my two brothers and I were numb. We each kept the deep grief to ourselves, each in a different way. For years, I secretly would have nightmares. Just as dust had begun to settle, we learned of the sudden death of our rector on the morning of my dad's anniversary, three years after presiding at his funeral.

I would attend daily morning Mass to start the day before going to work. The cathedral rector's ministry played a significant part in my beginning to find peace in the deaths of my mom and dad and to maintaining the faith in God that they had instilled in my brothers and me throughout our lives. When we find peace in the "passing" of our most loved ones, their love comes back to us in a much deeper form and in ways far beyond our innermost imaginings. I also found a peace in my own mortality. As I surrendered and dove deeper and deeper into my faith and love for God, I very physically felt a tiny glimpse of what being physically in God's presence and love must be like. During any given day, many unexplainable occurrences began to happen that could not possibly be coincidences. The only explanation I could derive at was that they were "God-incidences," being from a powerful energy frequency that is of God's love and very physical reminders that God is <u>always</u> right beside us.

During those years, my cousin's husband developed a debilitating illness. He was my closest and loved friend. It was painful to watch as the deterioration of his motor functions progressed. On Fridays, after morning mass, our group of church family and friends would go for breakfast. One morning, when he was beginning to struggle walking, we were leaving our regular restaurant in a building built in the 1920s. As he walked with another cousin in front of me around the corner of the building, he suddenly stopped. I, too, stopped, to keep from walking into him, and as I looked down to see if his legs looked okay, I noticed what appeared to be a medallion imbedded in the dirt and weeds where small piece of concrete was missing from the sidewalk up against the wall of the building. I reached down to pull it out of the ground and discovered it was a medal in the shape of a dog tag, heavily oxidized, and with an illegible engraving.

Obviously in the dirt many years, I wondered how no one had ever seen it with all the daily foot traffic there. After taking it home, and with cleaning and polishing, it was revealed that the engraving on the medal was the "Lord's Prayer." Prayer of all prayers. The following Friday at breakfast, I looked for the broken sidewalk from where I had pulled the medal from out of the hardened dirt; however, there was <u>no</u> broken or missing concrete and no signs of any new or repaired sidewalk. Emotions went down into my chest, and for a couple of weeks, I was without words. If my "buddy" hadn't stopped, I would not have seen the medal, so I figured the "sign" was intended for him and gifted him the medal with hopes of some kind of peace. He shared with me later that he carried it in his wallet.

In 2016, the illness took him from us, but it never took the awesome spirit and faith from him or from those of us who loved him. This guy, who had not been raised as a Catholic, had become a better "Catholic" than most lifelong Catholics I know. The following year, my cousin gifted me the medal from out of his wallet, and months later, a wooden crucifix from Costa Rica made from slices of small tree branches. The "branches" we all are on the "vine" of God. We don't know why God sends us "signals"; sometimes we don't even recognize them. All that is asked of us is to keep our hearts open to embrace them.

I mounted the medal onto the crucifix.

What is heartwarming relief, though, is that at the moment of death of each of our loved ones, there was invariably a peace in their faces and in the sudden stillness devoid of human worries and pain. In the midst of something divine and unexplainable that occurs at the moment of death, love... God's love, lifts the weight from the heavy, numbing air of human death with a "presence" and with the powerful manifestation of the sure existence of the "soul." Our "soul" exists in the highest form of energy within creation, God's living love. It is what puts that twinkle in our eye and the loving warmth in our hearts; it is what makes us each who we are and different from any other human being. It is what powers every cell in our one and only, individual, human body to live and function together as one of God's creations and part of His overall plan; all of which I was finally coming to understand more deeply. It literally holds our heart attached to the sacred heart of Jesus.

In all the "corniness" of all the "pious, religious stuff," an understanding began developing of the figurative, physical, and spiritual fact that we all have to die in order to live. I had noticed how my dad and loved ones in their last months or years had stopped worrying about all that superfluous "stuff," which we stubbornly shove, overstuff, and overload into our earthly duffle bags and arduously lug around on our shoulders and in our hearts all day long, every day, for years. As we begin to "let go" and surrender to God's "purpose" for us, we come to see kindness, patience, humility, and love in the reflections of the light of God more clearly.

God kisses our soul and in those deepest places within our hearts that only God can and will ever reach and touch and sends us into this world in the same way He Himself chose to come to us some two thousand years ago, as helpless, innocent, defenseless infants with nothing on our backs or in our hearts except His love. I believe God's mission and our purpose, is for us to return to Him in much the same way. And if we are blessed with lives well lived, we hopefully release and shed all the gunk, mutations, and biases our minds and hearts absorb during our earthly lives; to become who God created us to be. And just **maybe, <u>hopefully</u>**, our transformation occurs years before the flames of the candles of our earthly lives flicker away. Finding peace in my mortality, it was also confirmed to me that the REAL presence in the Eucharist is not simply a "belief" of Catholics but a true and undeniable "certainty."

But little did I know that I would soon allow the "Catholic religious" peace (<u>NOT</u> my spiritual peace) I thought I had found in a lifelong church for generations of family, friends and loved ones, to be destroyed by a new bishop and by many of our local diocesan clergy as they destroyed their credibility as priests to me, and as I struggled with the <u>repeated</u> callus lack of remorse of our diocese clergy in their clericalism, elitism, clerical abuses, and hurtful actions and behavior, as well as in the abuses that were unaccountably being exposed throughout our entire world Church which our diocesan clergy tried to downplay, pretend doesn't really happen, or pretend only happen "somewhere else"; "that kind of stuff doesn't happen here"! Worst of all, they try to deny they are even capable of any abuse and of inflicting harm.

My struggle with the harm that our diocesan clergy inflict with such hurtfulness and indifference is deeper than they will ever try or even care to selfishly understand.

A few months before our rector's unanticipated death in Chicago, our diocesan bishop had been transferred to California. A few months following our rector's death, Benedict had renounced his papacy. In the course of a few but long months, our world Church was without a pope. Our diocese was without a bishop, and our cathedral was without a rector or even an experienced parish priest. The young, inexperienced, recently ordained, seemingly loving and sincere priest at the cathedral was overwhelmed. For many days after our rector's death, the church family trekked to church every day to pray, some hoping for mutual support with a friendly face of our clergy, which never surfaced for mutual consolation with the parish community until after the rector's funeral, which was held in his hometown in Ohio. To attend the funeral of the one who was becoming his mentor was good for the mourning and personal closure of the young priest. He later shared with the congregation that he had been asked to dress our rector in his burial vestments and did not think he would have the strength to do so until he drew a peace from the still face, lying in the casket. He returned home stepping up to the plate and with a dedicated and promising potential for both the healing of the community and even more importantly, for his future ministry. The cathedral needed him, and he needed the cathedral, a few more months.

A new bishop, though, would soon arrive and unknowingly, seemingly uncaringly, derail that future potential that was in motion, away from him, the parish, the diocese, and the Church; destroy the healing process for the cathedral community; cause division and harm not only within the cathedral but throughout the diocese with future priest assignments; grandstanding his publicity and political positions on public TV, news, and social media rather than concentrating on the pastoral care of both laity and priests, and always lugging around his personal gold platted pedestal to be raised onto. And many oblige him. But in his own eyes, he seems to see himself as the "sun" of our diocese with hopes of a wider horizon.

That March of 2013, in Rome, Italy, six thousand miles away from El Paso, Jorge Mario Bergolglio was on the journey which was not of his own choosing, of being elected to be our next pope.

At the same time in Dallas, Texas, seven hundred miles away from El Paso, strategies for recommending to a new pope the hierarchal promotion for a tiny ignored corner in Texas were apparently in process. The new pope would be a modest unassuming man from Argentina, over five thousand miles away. The auxiliary bishop of Dallas, Texas, was Mark J. Seitz under Bishop Kevin Joseph Farrell. Farrell, the bishop of Dallas, had served as auxiliary bishop of Washington and had been consecrated to the position of bishop of

Dallas by their friend Cardinal Theodore McCarrick who in the coming months and years would be publicly exposed in one of the most disappointing and horrific scandals of clerical and sex abuse within our Church. McCarrick was a power broker in Washington circles and was an advisor through many connections in Rome and played part to the Vatican via recommendation letters to the popes for new bishops in the United States. Especially during a period when reports indicate conflicts brewing between him and the Apostolic Nuncio to the United States. In the summer of 2013, only a mere three months after Francis was elected to pope, Mark J. Seitz was promoted and assigned as bishop of El Paso. Traveling almost two thousand miles to be present and participate at his installation with great pomp was his friend Cardinal Theodore McCarrick, who according to various reports supposedly, due to the brewing scandal, was to have been remaining low profile and avoiding travel. Also traveling to El Paso to participate and to consecrate his friend was Bishop Kevin Farrell. In 2016, Farrell would not surprisingly be elevated to Cardinal, and in 2019 would be appointed as *Papal Carmerlengo* of the Church. All just coincidences? Maybe. But we can each with our God given intellects, deduce our own conclusions of what was evidently occurring behind the scenes and can begin to have an understanding of who the facilitators and <u>mentors</u> are to the clergy in charge of our neighborhood churches and who the poor <u>examples</u> are to our diocesan parish priests. Which of our bishops and priests in the United States are part of the "right wing" conservative clergy, who believe in the "<u>superiority and royalty</u>" of priests and who resist Vatican II, which threatens their pedestals? Perhaps we each have our own answer(s), part of which rests in our own authenticity, and in the depth of each of our faith and love for God.

There is an old saying in Spanish that in translation loses some of its sentiment: *"Dime con quien andas y te digo quien eres"; ["tell me who your friends are and who you hang around with, and I'll tell you who you are"]*.

None of us can ever claim to know what is in someone else's heart, but what each of us do know, is that who any of us associate with, does in fact impact our lives and patterns of behavior.

In more spiritual and profound words (translated from Spanish):

> *There is a saying (dicho)... Tell me how you pray and I will tell you how you live. Tell me how you live and I will tell you how you pray. For in showing me how you pray I will learn to discover the God you live. And in showing me how you live I will learn to believe in the God to whom you pray.* (Pope Francis in his homily in Morelia, Mexico, February 16, 2016)

This quote by Pope Francis is of huge profound relevance not solely to the lives of those of us of Catholic faith, but to the lives of those of <u>any</u> religion, <u>any</u> place in the world; for it is our faith, what we believe in, and how we pray, that impacts and defines how we live our lives; and perhaps even more importantly, <u>it is how we (including priests) live our lives that reflects what we believe in or what we don't believe in</u>.

Our new bishop was received and welcomed to El Paso with warm, open arms. To many, his well-attended installation was "hopeful." It did not take long, though, to see that he is not a warm and fuzzy man who lacked the simple courtesy of responding to correspondence or any show of gratitude or religious affection to many who sent him kind wishes and prayers. He was a "bishop" now! But he did not understand or knew and cared little if anything about the death and more importantly the **life** of our cathedral rector and disregarded the loss and mourning of the parish family, which was deeply in need of the healing process and some level of closure. During the period, when our diocese was without a bishop or cathedral rector, the Jesuit "religious" order were the only dependable clergy for regular daily masses; they could always be counted on. One morning during his first days in the diocese, the new bishop arrived unannounced for mass. Regardless whether it was a surprise visit or whether the office was notified in advance, the Jesuits were not informed, and our dependable Jesuit priest made the regular early morning trek to the cathedral. Rather than embracing and inviting the humble Jesuit to concelebrate and meet the new bishop, the new bishop and our young priest (who became available) "dismissed" him. The Jesuit humbly joined us in the pews. All in attendance were glad to meet our new "bishop," but those of us who were grateful to the Jesuits, recognized the "diocesan" selfishness and cold lack of courtesy. Should an **example** of warmth, caring, and communion between ALL clergy be **encouraged** and **expected**?

As the days and weeks progressed, unfamiliar with the culture, dynamics, clergy, laity, and the needs of the El Paso community(s) as a whole, the new bishop immediately began moving priests and assigning them without any support, where for various reasons they could not fit, and young priests to positions that require experience which brings mature wisdom to those roles, he exploited the more popular or politically active priests, he dismissed proactive religious order priests who perhaps "threatened" his direction and "claimed" pastoral and liturgical expertise and authority, he turned over the poorer "Hispanic" churches to the Religious Franciscan and Jesuit orders (unknowingly to the benefit of the parishes), and he assigned the dead rector's best friend as the new rector of the cathedral. The new rector, for whatever personal struggles already a difficult man to deal with, wrestling with his own personal issues and demons, and he himself deeply mourning, was now seemingly inconsiderately forced by the bishop to be immersed into the surroundings, the personal possessions, and to the constant critical comparisons to his dead best friend. In his farewell message in the bulletin of his previous parish, he apologized to anyone in the congregation who he may had hurt, which in itself should have been a sign to his "brotherhood" and of his reaching out for help. But most of diocesan "brotherhood" is only superficial. He was angry, bitter, impatient, always defensive and secretive, and often down right crude and hurtful—definitely not mellowed from the many years of experience he would often boast of serving as a "priest," criticizing rather than mentoring the lack of experience of "baby priests" as he would refer to them. All perhaps part of the pain and misery he may have been enduring within himself. When the bishop was around, the smile "mask" went on; behind the scenes, "defiance" ruled in the sad shadows of the insecurity of both men wanting "control."

We had all begun to feel the remarkable deterioration in the atmosphere of our church. I had never met him, though, until he was appointed as temporary administrator before becoming rector of the cathedral, and I went to meet with him as a witness for an upcoming family wedding, which is supposed to be a happy event in and for the church. As I was called in, it was obvious that he was furiously angry at someone or something. Waving both his arms in every direction with an ill-bred demeanor, he rudely signaled me into the room where we were to meet. I wondered to myself, *Wow, is this how the "face" of our cathedral now greets those who walk in through our doors reaching for kindness?*

When I turned to talk to him, he had disappeared without saying a word or excusing himself. As I walked into the room, I saw our young priest through the large sliding glass doors working outside in the one-hundred-plus degree heat of the sweltering summer afternoon. As we waved to each other and I walked toward the door, I felt a slap on my back and the angry priest telling me in Spanish to get away, that the young priest was being scolded and was "in time-out" as if he were a little boy and flippantly pointed me to an uncomfortable tiny table pushed against the corner of the large room. I've often wondered if I would have punched him if I hadn't been trying to be respectful and understand him better. Coupled with the gift of free will, God obviously gives men within the Catholic Church another gift that comes with learning to choose between right and wrong; that of the virtue of "restraint." He then opened the door, stuck his head out, and yelled something to the young priest who moved from public view. I tried to joke and lighten the mood, but he was carrying a barrier of rage in him that only got a smirk. After the meeting, I was "dismissed" out into the crowded waiting room, feeling a sense of anger and hurt from what I had just witnessed. A few minutes later, the young priest came out into the waiting room surprised to see so many in the crowded room. As he kindly greeted and hugged everyone one by one, he nervously turned and apologized to the wall he had backed into. I knew what was happening behind the scenes and could feel what he was going through behind his forced and uncomfortable smile. As he greeted me, I felt the humid sweat and intense heat that had been absorbed by his black clerics outside in the scorching sun and felt sorry and hurt for him.

I don't have any idea what had happened earlier and perhaps the older priest's anger was justified but not his uncontrolled "unpriestly" behavior. Since he was always angry and rude at someone every time we would see him at church, as frustrated as he would make me, I kept feeling sorry for him, kept forgiving him, and kept praying for him. The bishop soon published the notice that this man was becoming the rector and the young priest was being moved. I sent a message to the new rector that I had been angry at him for how he treated our young priest, that I needed peace and wanted to apologize and hoped he would apologize to the young priest on behalf of the parish and embrace him. He responded angrily and uncaringly, not accepting my apology and denying everything, including ever having the meeting at the cathedral and the young priest ever being present but rudely told me, "*If it brings you peace, good for you.*" With every day, it would become more and more difficult for me to accept how many who participated at church feared him and would avoid him if possible; some would even leave in angry tears. A few lay ministers would even avoid serving at mass with him. Why wouldn't they ever say anything or stand up to him; or why wouldn't those closest to him, or his "brothers" help him? Why are diocesan clergy so self-consumed, indifferent, and oblivious to others? The coming years, augmented with his arrogant "power-filled" assistant and fueled by our new bishop, would be very divisive and harmful for the cathedral.

Those who had known him for many years say that this new "rector" was once a kind priest. Somewhere along his walk, though, his ministry had sadly turned into a journey of misery casting dark harmful shadows which clergy are blind to. Also sadly, his "fraternity" brothers are too self-consumed to ever have helped him or whoever was hurt. The once-thriving cathedral where one would not long ago have to arrive early if one wanted to find a seat for Mass and where anyone who might be unhappy with the Church or complain, had to be careful because they would be welcomed and invited to participate and get deeper involved began to dwindle. Sunday collections significantly reduced. Longtime members of the church began leaving one by one either not returning to church altogether or making the rounds from church to church settling on a place hoping to feel at home. A thriving cathedral destroyed by one man's lack of leadership. **In the years to come, empty pews and apathy would be blamed on the COVID pandemic rather than the true cause: deep failures of our diocesan leadership and clergy.**

For many years prior, the rector of the cathedral was carefully picked, and the cathedral was the first assignment for every recently ordained young priest. But the new bishop did not understand and ignored the dynamics and the division, upheaval, and damage occurring in the pews and behind the scenes at the cathedral and surrounding churches and to the ministry of our priests as a result of his inexperienced chest pounding actions and his previous years in a wealthier diocese where almost no priest struggles with English. He ignored and dismissed the hurtful, abusive bullying going on behind the scenes toward our young new priests, seminarians, and laity by clergy (whether or not intentional). He ignored and dismissed the hurtful behavior of diocesan clergy and lack of pastoral care that he himself was part of and leading. He ignored and dismissed the liturgical example the cathedral should be for all parishes in the diocese and to what was being promoted at times contrary to the Roman Missal, Canon Law, and especially to "Sacrosanctum Concilium" (Vatican II), which have profound significance in our Church rituals. He could ignore whatever and whoever he chose while he flexed the muscles of his bishop *mitre* and played to a new false sense of power and his need of celebrity public perception. No one else matters. No one else's opinions matter unless they agree with his.

Soon after his arrival to El Paso, at his first ordination, I could not understand how a new bishop would so often go off standing alone with so many gathered for the event, or why he was interacting with the crowd so "distantly." I went to greet him. I had sent him a letter he never even acknowledged, welcoming him to EP, thanking him for celebrating mass with us during his first days, describing what our community was experiencing with our rector's sudden death, the great job our young priest was doing, and how the community needed him a few more months for <u>mutual</u> healing rather than the loss of another priest so soon. As I began greeting him, he very rudely turned his back and walked away. I realized that this is what had been occurring with any member of the "mere" laity if one was sharing information, expressing an opinion, and wasn't just telling him how "wonderful" he was while cameras "clicked." Whether it was arrogance or insecurity, it became obvious in the following months, that laity members are not welcome or "allowed" to discuss a differing viewpoint or concern with him. He seems to believe in the unworthiness, lack of intelligence, and religious inferiority of laity, and in **blind obedience** by <u>anyone</u> below the rank of "bishop." And he handles his "public" mask(s) well. Perhaps it was what impressed him and what he had learned from his friend McCarrick. What better mentor to show aspiring clergy what it takes to climb the hierarchical ladder with the illusion of "power" and "holy greatness." The **"McCarrick virus"** will one day prove to be just as contagious and **<u>fatal</u>** to priesthood and to <u>many</u> "religious" lives as the COVID virus has been to physical lives.

So many of us already knew what was occurring especially at the cathedral. But I could not comprehend why God would place me alone on multiple occasions with priests to witness how indifferent and hurtful one priest can be to another priest, seminarian, minister, or member of the laity; witness what they will say and do behind each other's backs; and worst of all, to watch them pretend nothing ever happened with too much pride to ever apologize to anyone. Why should I also be one to witness and live through how new young priests will cower, lacking physical and spiritual backbone for their vocation(s), purpose of priesthood, and those they are supposed to serve, and after someone stands up and defends them, to themselves be hurtful, judgmental, and indifferent with the "religious" scale tilted toward their self-interest and narcissism, and obligations to their bishop and fraternal brothers. Unfortunately, many diocesan priests really believe that "priesthood" is all about them rather than about those they are presumably "called" to serve for the cause of God. Even if a priest were to miraculously himself stand up for a victim, or confront or correct another priest, behind the scenes they are known to tell each other *"Who are you to judge me!"* or *"Don't interfere in my parish!"* Canon Law and misinterpreted scripture supports them. In addition, priest seniority and personal standing within the "fraternity" trumps priestly behavior amongst diocesan priests. So they avoid conflict amongst themselves and in doing so inflict additional harm to victims. The easy way out is for them to support their fraternity brother with the response to victims: ***"That is too bad," "That's just the way he his," and "Just pray for him,"*** rather than helping to fix a wrong and heal the heart wrenching pain they foster into a continuing cycle; and which they will never even try to understand or merely show compassion for. Unfortunately, the abusive clericalism that is throughout the diocese harms the entire Church. Many believe that from an Easterly facing window of our diocesan chancery office, "eyes" have a glowing "view" and focus to the Vatican.

Our young priest had astutely recognized that there was something to the ministry of our previous rector in how he got the attention of the congregation, interacted, and drew them to him. He had admitted in his homilies that he had always been very stubborn and an introvert and had once told the rector he wished he could be more like him when in front of people. He had begun imitating our rector's style of speaking to the congregation and his style of walking away from the ambo and up the pew aisles during his homilies where parishioners saw an endearing attempt.

As our bishop published his first new disruptive priest assignments, he added messages that there should be no attachments between the priest and the laity, and that priests should completely disengage. Every parish "branch" belongs to a separate "vine." In his distorted eyes, relationships between a priest and parishes were evidently to be superficial, abrupt, and temporary. Perhaps the reason why he carries around an icy barrier shield to separate himself from the flock, blatantly shakes and flaunts his mitre in front of him and handles his bishop's staff like an ice pick on the floor whenever he walks up the chilly unwelcoming church aisle.

But prior to the announcement being made public our young priest obviously had already been notified he would be leaving, for there was a noticeable change in his demeanor. After masses, he began to pick and choose who he would give time to, who he would "dismiss," and who he would exclude from one of his many "cliques" he was beginning to form. One evening after mass, I was standing nearby when the expressions on the faces of an elderly couple got my attention as they approached. There was a reason only they knew why they were there that day. The woman, obviously enduring some spiritual or personal pain, appeared to feel that he was the one she wanted to talk to. But appearing bothered, he simply asked the couple what parish they were from and told them to go and talk to their parish priest. As I watched them turn and walk away, her husband put his arm around her and embraced her, both their faces downcast. A part of my heart walked out with them. I could feel some of their pain and wondered how their lives would be affected by that very simple act of indifference and turning his back on them. Something that over the years has proven to come easier and easier for him, thanks to "his" bishop and fellow priests who all thrive on their self-interest, and indifference to others, and who are glaring examples to vulnerable young men "learning" how to be "priests" the wrong way.

When the announcement of the cathedral's young priest leaving was made public, a part of him in a sense also "died," as "disengagement" and indifference became more obvious. For he immediately disappeared to take time off, returning for his final week before starting his new assignment, but bulletin notices advised that he would not be available to meet with members of the congregation. Our diocesan clergy constantly demonstrate that "church" is just a **"business."**

Our new bishop had derailed the maturing process of a loving, spiritual ministry that was developing within the mourning cathedral family and community. But as our young priest was "dismissed" from his "family" into the next phase of his "diocesan life," it became obvious that there was something missing—something that can't be imitated or learned in books, something that begins at home with nurturing parents and a loving family and continues in the formation process within our seminaries then magically develops over time with loving mentors, experience, prayer, and a heart as big and authentic as one's vocation. Something very sad was happening. When he had started trying to be like the rector who everyone admired and began to learn how to work the crowds, he began to shed his own endearing identity to become who others wanted him to be, who he thought he was supposed to be, and what he was wrongly learning a priest is supposed to be through the eyes of his "bishop" and "adoring groupies," and to climb the ranks. The "mentor" who had started him onto a narrower, better path had **died**.

One year on a family cruise vacation, there was a famous older actress and a famous young singer on board. The actress was brought in by helicopter for her performance, and the singer was one of the passengers relaxing with her family. One afternoon, we met the singer with her family; surprisingly, my dad didn't know who she was, but with genuine warmth, she lovingly embraced him as if they were related or had known each other for years. Years later, I found that she had been going through a serious health diagnosis; her kindness was authentic. The actress, on the other hand, came down to greet the audience one evening after her performance. I was confronted with her face inches away from mine. Her glassy-eyed expression with a frozen, almost-plastic expression and smile on her face left an impression on me that I will never forget. It was her "public" face, the one she more than likely had rehearsed for many years and wore for the adoring crowds. During a large, very crowded gathering at the end of his next "assignment," where many were trying to reach out to him, I saw a similar expression on the face of our young priest. His ministry was starting to have to <u>adjust to the "actor"</u> that transforms and distorts personalities, and to **becoming a "celebrity" rock stars that <u>dooms Catholic priests.</u>**

> *"We are so accustomed to disguise ourselves to others, that in the end, we become disguised to ourselves"* (François de La Rochefoucauld).

In my initial short conversations with him after he had been ordained, I fully believed that he had the ability and sincere desire to be a good priest. He was also a victim to how a significant death and event at the cathedral of the diocese was poorly handled. But what happens in seminaries to obviously good men? Perhaps learning to be an "actor" and chasing the insulated comfort of exalted life of diocesan priesthood is part of "Seminary 101." Perhaps "priesthood" allows them to hide who God made them and to be shaped into the "diocesan" mold. Only they and God know. But with our young priest's charm, charisma, and high intellect, if he had just been himself, had been "allowed" to be himself, developed his own style of reaching out to the spiritually thirsty pews, and tried to humbly be who God created him to be. Our previous rector once said that this priest had the peace he had never seen in a recently ordained priest. All but a couple of his fellow priests had thrown him under the bus after the death of our rector; a few even seemed jealous that a young man recently out of the seminary was temporarily taking the helm of a "cathedral." It was extremely difficult to witness what I believed was a great potential as a priest being derailed by our new bishop and his fellow "brothers," quickly interrupting the maturing process that was being fast-tracked as he (I believed) tried to sincerely help with the huge loss and trauma, "mutually" occurring in the lives of our large extended church family.

I believed in his potential and something that seemed different from other priests. I trusted him. I felt sorry for him. I tried to provide support any way I could; on multiple occasions, I defended and stood up for him. He was one of the few diocesan priests one could feel comfortable talking with and being forthright and would be <u>one</u> of the clergy who would end up causing some of the greatest harm to me as a practicing Catholic. But many of us knew he had his struggles he was dealing with deep inside himself. As his assignments changed and his priestly self-worth continued to climb and heart slowly stiffened, he was the priest who was refusing to give the Eucharist to a young couple engaged to be married and who were living together for economic reasons or refusing out of self-pride to give a blessing, which someone asked him to give to a parishioner as mass was ending. In both cases, he hesitantly came through, but not without embarrassing and deeply hurting "human beings" in front of their church friends at Mass.

One Saturday morning, Mass was delayed thirty to forty-five minutes waiting for the television crews who he had coordinated to film portions of the Mass to be in the news; the cameras disrupted the Mass celebration and very obviously affects a priest's "performance." He never could understand, or cared to understand, why I had such strong issue with the clericalism and clerical abuses of our diocesan clergy and how they were with indifference adversely impacting those in the pews and with a bishop who obviously didn't care, even about his individual priests unless they support and promote his personal causes for "public" perception and reports to the Vatican. I continue to pray for our maturing priest that one day the face he sees in the mirror and the faces he wears on the altar and behind the scenes will be one and the same face God loving gifted him, with very specific intentions. What I do know is that the self-interest and "face" he has shown to some of us behind the limelight is not the one from God, and that the "face" I <u>know</u> God gave him is the only one that will fulfill God's calling to be a true loving priest for the cause of God.

Late one afternoon during a retreat, as the serenity of the evening crept in, I was walking alone with our new rector down the long hallway in the empty, dark, and deep quiet **peace** of the retreat center. I had previously left the retreat team and agreed to return but fatigued from the repeated hurt and frustration at church while weighing the conundrum that we may not like what someone does or how they behave, but we can still learn to love them and continue forgiving them. It is physically, mentally, and spiritually exhausting, though. In another building across the courtyard were over a hundred other men. As we reached the end of the darkening hallway dimly lit only by the setting sun and from the lighted library through a French door, our then current young priest, recently ordained, was visible peacefully silent on his knees in deep prayer, preparing for confessions. He was the only priest who had arrived on time and early enough to spiritually prepare himself.

As I thought to myself, *What an awesome image and source of grace for me in the retreat work ahead of us*, I could actually feel a "heat" from the fury of our rector next to me as I whispered *"Fr. ⸻ is praying."* As I began to reach out in disbelief and with the thought of restraining him, he had already rushed in. As the door slammed open, he yelled harshly, chastising the young loving priest over an issue of total and complete selfishness and bullying. As the "one in charge," he simply and selfishly had already in his own mind claimed rights to take that particular room for himself that night. The young priest, a large gentle man, jumped off the kneeler from his kneeling position to his feet, in what seemed to me was a foot in the air, with a loud shaking *thump!* on the old wooden floor. Both of us startled, he had already sensed my reaction and ignored the older priest for a moment, came over to me, put his hand on my shoulder, and looking me straight in the eyes, said gently, *"I'm okay, Rick."* It was something that came from his heart, not from any seminary. As he let me know what simple accommodations he needed to relocate for confessions and turned to try to calm and appease the tantrum of the furious priest, I walked out to give the two some privacy and to make sure no one was rushing from outside in who might have heard the yelling. I had been having problems with my blood pressure, and as I proceeded to one of the meeting rooms to do one of the readings for the retreat, something serious inside of me was occurring, affected my eyesight and physically the remainder of the evening and the coming years; the priest would never know or care how his repeated mistreatment of people affected others. But for that instant, I could very physically feel the peaceful presence of God behind one man and something evil behind the other.

Ironically, during one of our group meetings, one of the troubled attendees at the retreat stood up to say that even though he had never met the rector who was a *"little guy,"* that he *"was scared of him and glad that the large young priest was there to defend him if needed."* If the rector had been the only priest present, the Church would surely have lost one or more members.

When anyone, including a priest, is walking focused in the presence of God, it is quite obvious and inspiring. To this day, I continue to pray for that young priest that he may remain focused to God's presence around him, in spite of our diocese and arrogant fraternity brothers he ministers with and kindly accommodates while avoiding conflict.

As clergy get comfortable in their priestly "authority," abuses become more and more blatant, but the abuses are ignored by many because "they're priests." If one stands up to or reaches out to a member of the clergy for a wrong inflicted, it is easier for the clergy to turn their backs and walk away rather than to say **"I'm sorry"**—powerful yet difficult words when pride is involved.

The deeper we fall in love with God, the more our hearts soften, and we become loving, trusting, and vulnerable. Loving and trusting people of faith are very forgiving, even within a Church that continues to thrive in abusive clericalism, secrecy and lack of transparency.

"To err is human, to forgive is divine" (Alexander Pope).

So how many times do we, as Catholics, dig our heads into the sand, forgive, and continue to allow priest clericalism to inflict harm on others and to the Church over and over again?

> *"Then Peter approaching asked him, 'Lord... how often, must I forgive him? As many as seven times?' Jesus answered, 'I say to you, not seven times but seventy-seven times'"* (Matt. 18:21).

BUT to repeatedly dismiss priests, though, who show or express no sense of guilt, remorse, and compassion **is actually extremely septic and damaging to our entire Church.**

There's a story of a young man who is walking with his father. As they walk, the young man turns and asks his father, *"Dad, I want to get married."*

The father answered, "First tell me you're sorry."

Son: "For what?"

Father: "Say sorry."

Son: "But for what? What did I do?"

Father: "Just say sorry."

Son: "But...what have I done wrong?"

Father: "Say sorry."
Son: "WHY?"
Father: "Say sorry!"
Son: "Please dad, just tell me why?!"
Father: "Say sorry."
Son: "Okay, Dad… I'm sorry."
Father: "Finally! You've now finished your training. When you learn to say 'sorry' for no reason at all, then you're ready to get married!" (Author unknown).

The above story is just a joke of course. But we are all human. We all hurt others. Sometimes, unfortunately, hurt is done with the intention of hurting, but usually, hopefully, it is unintentional. There may even be times when we didn't even have an idea that we had hurt someone until they later bring it to our attention. When we realize we have hurt someone or it is brought to our attention, the love within us tells us to say *"I'm sorry I hurt you"* or *"I did not intend to hurt you, I'm really sorry,"* but to be sincere. Most importantly, we try to not hurt them again, especially not to hurt them "repeatedly." If one's status or position, especially as a member of the "clergy," makes one actually believe he can do no wrong, or one's pride does not allow them to say "I'm sorry" or even to recognize someone's hurt, what a shame, for that in itself, is I believe, a self-separation from Christ.

At two separate retreats, discussions arose over the deep pain and even some anger of some of the faithful (attendees) who had gone to confession. Priests, one a "bishop," had refused to grant them absolution because they believed they still had "issues" and more importantly because they "know they can." The young men described how they had sincerely been working on some personal issues they had but were truly remorseful. Clergy had judged what was in someone else's heart and refused absolution to those who were sincerely sorry while clergy themselves <u>demand</u> repeated forgiveness for what they <u>refuse to acknowledge and to be sorry for</u>. To arrogantly refuse absolution to anyone without knowing what is in one's heart inflicts <u>grave</u> harm. I had always assumed it probably did not ever occur much and had never given refusal of absolution much thought until listening to a member of our church family describe his confessional experience with his voice trembling and the need to clear his throat. As he sat down, I could hear him quietly mutter, *"It really hurt."* The priest heading the retreat acknowledged that he himself had once also been loudly scolded at confession before he entered ranks of the priesthood, and made a hypocritical comment, *"Some priests can be jerks!"* As a diocesan priest, he is one of the "fraternity" brothers who runs and hides from conflict.

Does one need to be a "priest" to call another priest a "jerk"? Absolutely not. There are a lot of "those" in our Church. Most laity, though, will never be forthright with a "priest," it goes with the intimidation and overpiousness of laity and the inherent "clericalism" of our clergy. But what is the end result from a "priest" who only stands up behind their backs to gain points from an audience, <u>pretending</u> to be their supportive "friend"?

The history of the Catholic Church in the United States as it evolved within the world Church, has many dark corners, shadows, and stains. Our US clergy have enjoyed their false sense of "holy," "royalty," and "caste" system within the institution of our Church which is much of the underlying cause of abuses throughout our Church. Through failure of our bishops, "shepherds" and "sheep" have been reverting to the pre-Vatican II Latin Mass, which supports and promotes that clericalism. The congregation is required to <u>read</u> the translated liturgy in order to follow along and are not active participants but <u>only</u> observers to the presiding priest who gives his back to them and where women "are considered not worthy" at the altar and must wear veils on their heads. In an effort for inclusiveness within the Church, Pope John Paul II in 1988 issued *"Ecclesia Dei"* to establish a commission after an archbishop was excommunicated for creating four bishops without papal authority. It allowed for conservative clergy maintaining communion with Rome and loyalty to the papacy.

In 2007, Pope Benedict with some shortsightedness, issued his Motu Propio *"Summorium Pontificum"* allowing traditional pre-Vatican II Latin liturgy with specific conditions. In 2014, soon after becoming bishop of El Paso, Mark Seitz, who is obviously one of our conservative US bishops, <u>invited</u> the Priestly Fraternity of St. Peter (FSSP) to move into one of El Paso's historic churches, for the purposes of celebrating pre-Vatican II liturgy. A box of veils for women to borrow and the list of church "rules" at the front door, now greeted the "faithful." In his lack of knowledge of the city and requesting no input from the community, the bishop "took away" a beloved church, which for almost a century, many would walk from downtown offices and businesses to mass, confessions, or just to pray during the day. The bishop also allowed a daily Latin mass at the cathedral. The new "sect" has caused religious confusion to members of the faithful and division throughout the diocese. In the months to follow during a Chrism Mass, with most of our priests present, it was self-explanatory how the FSSP priest who was present, "was allowed" to remain in the pews rather than following his "brothers" up to the altar to concelebrate, and to where they brought the Eucharist to <u>him</u>. While Canon Law does not make concelebrating mandatory, the perception was nonetheless that of priestly arrogance. It is interesting, as reported in June of 2021, that the priests of the Fraternity of St. Peter (FSSP) were expelled from the archdiocese of Dijon in Eastern France for <u>refusing</u> to concelebrate in post Vatican II liturgy (*"Novus Ordo"*). In the spirit of "communion" and "unity" in the Catholic Church, **<u>why</u>** would priests refuse to concelebrate? Perhaps it is an attempt to defend an exalted priestly "status," to refuse to understand and accept, and to defy the entire <u>purpose</u> of Vatican II. Many members of the laity who support the pre-Vatican II liturgy are either ultra conservative or are sentimental to "memories" of church of their youth. It is obvious that many do <u>not</u> understand the intent of Vatican II, with a denial and a significant cost to the more humble and inclusive teachings of Jesus. Fortunately, on July 16, 2021, efforts to stop defiance to Vatican II were promulgated by Pope Francis through his Motu Propio "Taditionis Custodes." The Fraternity of St. Peter, however, asked Pope Francis to be allowed to continue their "practices" and on February 2022 Francis <u>politely</u> has allowed them by decree but with conditions that bishops and priests have failed to explain publicly. The Fraternity of St. Peter is being allowed to continue with the roman missal in effect in 1962 but *"**<u>only</u>** in their <u>own</u> churches or oratories"* and also *"in the celebration of **<u>private</u>** masses."* In the decree, Pope Francis VERY POLITELY and CLEARLY suggested *"that, as far as possible, **the provisions of** the **motu proprio Traditionis Custodes be taken into account** as well,"* which has profound implications of intentions for our Church and for its reform.

Perhaps Pope Francis was being respectful of Benedict's papacy, but Pope Francis obviously believes in a Church that is "inclusive" and (I believe) that in his loving spirit, he "wants" to trust his "priests." Nevertheless, Francis **continues** to implore each and every member of the Church to follow the teachings of Jesus and to allow oneself to be enlightened to the intent of Vatican II, in the ongoing reform of our Church. Yet many arrogant ultra conservative clergy, with their prideful clericalism, continue to oppose Francis, even to the extent of claiming that the Motu Propio decree by Pope Francis does <u>NOT</u> need to be obeyed.

Does reverting to pre Vatican II liturgy serve to promote "priests" to strive to become "holy" examples of the more humble teachings of Jesus? Or does it serve more to the self-interests and exaltation of conservative priests? Many, will hide from the true answer.

On May 7, 2022, Pope Francis with his *relentless* faith and speaking to teachers and students of the Pontifical Liturgical Institute repeated how **Vatican II** verified the *"need of the people of God to live and participate more intensely in the liturgical life of the Church,"* and decried the resistance of *"closed mindsets"* to the reform of the Church using the liturgy for divisiveness in the Church with the *"odour of the devil, the deceiver."* In my opinion, ONLY with true belief in Jesus and in His mission, can one embrace the Motu Propio "Taditionis Custodes" by Pope Francis, and in the hope of reducing harmful clericalism and abusive priestly lifestyles within the Catholic Church. The Priestly Fraternity of St. Peter was established in 1988 with twelve priests. In 2022, there are approximately 340 priests and 180 seminarians worldwide. It is understandable why "priests" would desire to join the fraternity, for it promotes clericalism, the false sense of royalty, and the exaltation of "priests." But for laity to choose to practice their "Christian" faith by reverting to pre-Vatican II can only be with ignorance to the teachings of Jesus and to His mission, and as Francis described, with *"closed mindsets"* to the reform of the Church.

Arrogant self-referential bishops and members of the clergy, **who REFUSE to be humbled**, are worldwide. But we have more than our share within the United States and even within our local diocese(s). And ALL of them are raised up and sustained onto their pedestals by overpious laity blinded by the clericalism of "men," simply because they happen to be "priests."

In September of 2019, Pope Francis was quoted, *"It's an honor if the Americans attack me."* As American "Catholics," we should all understand his disappointment and the reason for his comment, and **we should all feel ashamed**.

Cardinal Theodore McCarrick has been one of the more conservative bishops in our Church. The report released by the Vatican in November 2020 as well as various accounts by victims, focuses on sexual abuses, but they describe clerical abuses by McCarrick at **many** levels. In accounts following a sex abuse where he had involved another priest, the two "priests" administered the sacrament of confession to each other, absolved each other, and then he later celebrated Mass. Did they know what was in each other's hearts? They more than likely did, and so did God. Thank God, however, that those confessions are confidential. No one should even **want** to know what they said to each other. Even after being credibly accused, he is reported to have continued extensive travel to over twenty or so countries, traveling anywhere the pope was going to be; and he continued to receive permission to perform church duties, including ordaining priests and following through with his recommendations for bishop promotions. In the few years McCarrick was in Newark and Washington, DC, he is reported to have sent millions of dollars he raised, many times passing around envelopes during his visits to Rome buying him hierarchical contacts, support, and power within the church. He was wined and dined as a "holy celebrity" with political leaders for fundraisers and with many who considered it "prestigious" to know him. All greater magnitudes of the same precursor abuses we see in our local dioceses by our local bishops and clergy, and all abuses most of the laity keep quiet to, come to believe are part of being "Catholic" and continue to support and promote. This exalted "priest" and poor example of a man who was treated as a "celebrity" even by presidents is the abusive cardinal we've all seen on national TV, read about in the news, and who has seriously harmed our <u>entire</u> Church. But he has definitely negatively impacted our local diocesan and worldwide clergy through his example as a priest, bishop, archbishop, and cardinal, more than we can imagine or they might admit. Men impressed by his position, "power," and clericalism within the hierarchy of our vulnerable Church. He has since been "defrocked," but in all his public statements, he continues to deny abusive shame he has inflicted on "priesthood," and **refuses** to remorsefully say two simple words to the Catholic world: **"I'm sorry."**

Meantime, the many bishops and "priests" he has been an example to and impressed, continue their quest toward the golden "throne" of Peter, a man-made "illusion," which corrupts weak, power-thirsty men. Jesus **never** gave Peter a "throne." The "throne" is the aspiration of human bishops. Personal aspirations and the self-interest of our clergy destroy the entire <u>purpose</u> and <u>credibility</u> of "priesthood" and to moving the mission of Christ <u>forward</u> as a "religion."

> *"Do you* [we] *not yet understand or comprehend? Are your* [our] *hearts hardened? Do you* [we] *have eyes and not see; ears and not hear? And do you* [we] *not remember?" (Mark 8:17–18).*

The "misdirection" begins and is nurtured in our seminaries.

Deacons and Seminarians

In November of 2019, while speaking to the Vatican's Dicastery for Laity, Family, and Life in regard to permanent deacons in our Church, Pope Francis warned against the danger of *"clericalizing the laity."* Sometimes, he said, permanent deacons who are to be the custodians of service in dioceses soon find themselves *"looking at the altar"* and end up as *"wannabe priests."* Francis said deacons should not become slaves to the clergy and to ***"move deacons away from the altar... *** *They are guardians of service, not first-class altar boys or second-class priests."* He was crystal clear that deacons are not called to serve bishops and priests but to serve the Church and to evangelize, which is why by Canon Law they proclaim the gospel at mass. On June 19, 2021, Pope Francis reiterated the role of permanent deacons in the Church.

But contrary to directives from Pope Francis, our local bishop continues to exploit our deacons in their service to him and clergy nurturing clericalism. The word *deacon*, from the Greek "diakonos" means "servant," but servants to who? Our deacons fill in for the convenience of our priests at communion services and other duties; and deacons or funeral lay ministers will preside at most of funeral vigil services except for high-profile church members. Whether or not they are serving as "deacons" with sincerity, they don't seem to even realize or care that they are serving as exploited slaves and "servants" to the clergy. Our deacons come to believe that they are "in persona 'priests,'" and enjoy their "elevated," "semipriestly" roles on the altar. Our bishop's Mass "performances" come with an entourage of deacons, priests, altar servers, "performers and backup singers," and cameras. Our deacon assigned to the cathedral follows the bishop and "concelebrates" at <u>multiple</u> Sunday masses, regardless of the parish, and the bishop and deacon often wear identical chasubles and vestments. The deacons perform the duties that Francis clearly warns the world about "*first-class altar boys* [and] *second-class priests,*" as the quiet altar servers are pushed to the corner and behind the altar rather than being <u>lovingly</u> included and embraced to share as full participants at mass. Deacons begin to believe they shine their own "light" and come to falsely believe that their level of "clericalism" is serving the mission of Christ. Pope Francis clearly explains the **purpose** of the "deacon" very <u>differently</u>, to deaf ears.

The El Paso diocese has a preseminary which is regularly incorrectly referred to as a seminary. Young men out of high school are recruited (not "inspired"), with many being from other less fortunate countries. Before they are sent on to seminaries, many are sent to local colleges to learn English, which the diocese does not follow up with or nurture to inspire fluency. A preseminarian one afternoon shared with me his disappointment in the lack of spiritual discussions with the priests and about witnessing how another who had a change of heart or had to leave had been treated like an outcast. The preseminarians are utilized as altar servers and church assistants rather than in a more involved formation process. During the bishop's early years, since they were posted on Facebook and church websites, preseminarians were obviously assigned to take pictures and videos of the priest, including during the consecration, during weekly Mass celebrations <u>rather</u> than being trained to be fully "present participants" and to **focus** on the powerful sacrament occurring on the altar. I once felt compelled to tell a preseminarian who was manning the rectory front desk and phone, to smile and be friendly to people, and to answer the phone with kindness. The diocese very obviously does **not** believe that kind reception, whether physically at the front office or via the phone, is a very important part of the "ministry." When they're sent on to out of town seminaries, they leave with the bad habits they've picked up from the local priests, learning to aspire for and love the pedestal they've watched them be raised onto by the laity. Preseminarians and seminarians can be seen in awe as they watch priests who have only been ordained a couple of years be wined and dined, and traveling every year on world "pilgrimage" vacations, with the anticipation of they themselves soon having that luxury. One evening after mass I found it disappointing to hear a **PRE-**seminarian describe what he would be wearing when he would become pope.

In November of 2017, our diocesan preseminary posted the following:

> *When you think that not even the Blessed Virgin can do what a priest does.*
>
> *When you think that not even the angels, nor the archangels, nor Michael or Gabriel or Rafael, nor any of those who defeated Lucifer, can do what a priest does.*

When you think that Our Lord Jesus Christ at the Last Supper performed a miracle greater than the creation of the Universe with all its splendor and transformed the bread and wine into His Body and Blood to feed the world, and that this event, before which angels and men kneel, a priest can repeat every day.

When you think of the other miracle that only a priest can perform: forgive sins and what he binds at the bottom of his humble confessional, God bound by his own word, binds him in heaven, and what he unties, at the same moment God unties it.

When one thinks that humanity has been redeemed and that the world subsists because there are men and women who feed each day on that Body and that redeeming Blood that only a priest can fulfill.

When one thinks that the world would die of the worst hunger if it were to lack that little bit of bread and that little bit of wine.

When one thinks that this can happen, because priestly vocations are lacking; and that when that happens the skies will be shaken and the Earth will explode, as if the hand of God had stopped sustaining it; and people will cry out of hunger and anguish, and they will ask for that bread, and there will be no one to give it to them; and they will ask for the absolution of their faults, and there will be no one to absolve them, and they will die with their eyes open for the greatest of frights.

When you think that a priest is more important than a king, more than a soldier, more than a banker, more than a doctor, more than a teacher, because he can replace everyone and none can replace him.

When one thinks that a priest when celebrating at the altar has a dignity infinitely greater than a king; and that it is not a symbol, not even an ambassador of Christ, but that it is Christ himself who is there repeating the greatest miracle of God.

When you think about all this, you understand the immense need to foster priestly vocations. One understands the eagerness with which, in ancient times, each family longed for a priestly vocation to sprout from its bosom, like a rod of nard. One understands the immense respect that people had for priests, which is reflected in the laws. One understands that the worst crime anyone can commit is to prevent or discourage a vocation. One understands that to cause apostasy is to be like Judas and sell Christ again. One understands that if a father or a mother obstructs the priestly vocation of a son, it is as if they renounce a title of incomparable nobility. One understands that more than a Church, and more than a school, and more than a hospital, it is a seminary or a novitiate. One understands that

giving to build or maintain a seminary or a novi-
tiate is to multiply the births of the Redeemer. One
understands that giving to pay for the studies of a
young seminarian or of a novice is to pave the way
for a man to reach the altar who for half an hour,
every day, will be much more than all the dignities
of the earth and all the saints of heaven, because it
will be Christ himself, sacrificing his Body and his
Blood, to feed the world. (Author unknown)

The above posting was removed after a few weeks; I like to hope after receiving objections. Unfortunately, based on the attitudes and behavior patterns of clergy and candidates within the diocese, it is an indication and very telling of what the diocese was sadly and unfortunately promoting to seminarians and to how clericalism and elitism is fostered so early in their priesthood. What a religious shame to our Church. It is interesting that many of the recently ordained priests now wear heavy, floor-length capes which they believe represent royalty and that they actually <u>believe</u> clericalism is minimal or absent in the diocese.

One of the most recent announcements by the bishops of the United States in October of 2021 was the new requirement that young men entering the seminary will need to be willing to have DNA samples or detailed medical exams to ensure that transgender seminarians don't make it through the cracks (since one candidate evidently almost did). The issue of transgender, homosexual, or "other" in the priesthood is a complex political, ethical, and moral discussion for another forum, but for the purposes here, though, I

6

believe the bigger problem is that it very obviously exemplifies that our church leadership <u>itself</u> acknowledges that <u>those applying for the "priesthood" cannot be trusted</u> and doubts that any information in their applications is truthful and with full disclosure. Lack of truthfulness, transparency, and even of perhaps morality within the Church very obviously begins when the young men apply to the seminaries for priesthood.

When the "kids" enter the preseminary, many are immature teenagers who were living in insulated and even dysfunctional lives. When they return from out of town Seminaries, some have been mentored, touched and inspired by a good example seminary priest, only to struggle implementing into the local dysfunctional diocesan environment. Others obviously are not inspired at all. A minority will hopefully one day become good priests. But by the time they are ordained and become priests, most have never held a job and would have a difficult time surviving in the real world, understanding that "real" world and what people and families go through in their everyday lives, without handouts. Like their mentors, it is rare to ever offer a helping hand for any "menial" work within the church or to laity, especially when it is <u>not</u> convenient for them.

In January 2014, a few months after Francis became pope, he met privately with 120 superiors of religious orders. The Vatican seems to have avoided publishing any summary of that meeting, but comments of the meeting were published by the Civilta Cattolica, an Italian Jesuit Journal. Pope Francis was described as having talked passionately and bluntly about the formation of priests and clericalism. How young men need to be properly trained in seminaries; that their hearts need to be formed, or run the risk of creating priests who are **_"little monsters."_** That _"the men arrive to seminaries gritting their teeth, smiling a lot, and just following the rules, so that they will be ordained."_ How religious life should not be an escape for them, a hiding place, to seek a comfortable place with emphasis on their careers and climbing the hierarchy rather than taking care of the Church. Francis was quoted as believing strongly that priests needed to reach out to the peripheries of society so that they may become acquainted with the reality and life experiences of the people they serve. Seminary classes can't teach that. Francis's very astute evaluation of the failure of our seminaries is "right on point" at our preseminary.

In the EP Diocese, after a few years of study the young men are given their pedestals and scepters (in the form of their collars) for their coronation (ordination). Clericalism begins in the preseminary years before they are crowned. Once ordained, though, after a few years in seminary all the young new priests, many who are introverts and who a few weeks earlier may have even avoided speaking to members of the laity, are considered experts in human lives and experts in all things "spiritual" and to "God," which no one is. Most of these young men have never learned the full meaning of personal sacrifices for those one deeply loves. They are given their church assignment(s) to fend for themselves without much mentorship and with no real accountability. And they are immediately revered by laity of whom the reverence is expected and sometimes demanded. One thing our seminaries sadly do very well is to teach our young priests' presentation and how to utilize the collar for public perception of "holiness," early in the formation process. The perception of "humbleness," requires "practice," as the "actor" develops.

When the clerical status begins to feel comfortable and forms arrogance (in most cases) usually within the first two years of priesthood, the load of carrying around two faces becomes lighter and almost second nature. Eventually, though, and usually behind the scenes, one of the faces they carry, the face that God did not create and give them, surfaces to a "victim." Through their actions, words, and lifestyles, their hurtful or abusive lifestyles progress and clergy begin to destroy their credibility as "priests." Especially as one witnesses opportunistic clergy rise within the "hierarchy" of the Church, which was **never** part of the mission of Christ.

The hierarchy was originally initiated almost two centuries after the crucifixion of Jesus for unity within the Church to ensure consistency between the many different communities that were beginning to sprout and grow after Christianity was legalized. Large organizations require control, but "hierarchy" has evolved with a blackened heart of its own as a means for human authority and sense of power of position and "title" among bishops. Initially within the Church, priests, "presbyters," were only assistants to the bishops who were not allowed to administer the Eucharist or other sacraments. As more church communities began to sprout, priests were allowed to administer communion with permission of the bishop. The church soon realized they also needed a pool from which more bishops could be created. This is one of the reasons only bishops can ordain priests. The hierarchy, though, has become a false "power" structure in the church. For many priests, it is actually a "**climb up into hell.**"

It is unfortunate, that soon after ordination, many of the new young priests can so easily (and perhaps encouraged), to avoid pastoral care by immediately embarking into doctorate programs in

Canon Law, scripture, or theology, not for continuing spiritual growth or discernment, but rather to be eligible in the pool for promotions within the ecclesiastical hierarchy of the Church to become a "bishop" by the time they reach the minimum thirty-five years of age, per Canon 378.

It is reflective in the demeanor of <u>any</u> "bishop" whose promotion and position occurred humbly without he himself aspiring for and actively pursuing the personal "climb" within the hierarchy. After being elected as pope, Francis referred to his "papacy" as his "penance."

Ironically, in 2016, a few days after Valentine's Day, Pope Francis joyfully brought his heart to the Mexican city of Juarez along the border with El Paso. God blessed a few of us "laity" to meet, transport, and get to know visiting bishops, archbishops, and cardinals from across the United States. It was interesting to see which bishops did not insist on crossing the border into Mexico to try to be seen with or to impress the pope and who participated on the US side.

For myself, while enduring the anguish of being discouraged and disillusioned from the church I love by the diocesan clergy of El Paso, it was a source of hope to see and experience firsthand that clergy **do** exist in the upper ranks of our Church hierarchy who **do** try to carry Christ's mission forward and who **do** attempt to live their religious lives as authentically as they can, given the structure of the institution of our Church. A couple have even proven that in their rise in the hierarchy that they have continued to nurture their hearts humbly enough to graciously remember laity (who are not even of their dioceses) by name, whose paths crossed with theirs, for years to come, with signs of appreciation and with warm kindness, with God's love, and with sincerity.

Fr. Ron Rolheiser, an Oblate priest and theologian, in his reflections reminds us that **"hope trumps over cynicism."** I continue to pray for that victorious hope in our Church.

> *"And hope does not disappoint, because the love of God has been poured out into our hearts through the Holy Spirit that has been given to us"* (Rom. 5:5).

In that excerpt from his letters in chapter 5 of Romans, St. Paul uses a metaphor of God's love flowing like a liquid. We already have God's love in us when we were created. The love keeps overflowing to us no matter how much or how many times we might at times hurt God by hurting others. It's comforting to know that whatever love our clergy do not embrace, continues to flow and be available for anyone with open arms and a loving heart.

> *"Each one of us, is a story of the love of God. God calls each of us by name... The Resurrection of Jesus is not a joy given with an eyedropper, but a cascade, a waterfall that fills our whole life"* (Pope Francis, May 17, 2017).

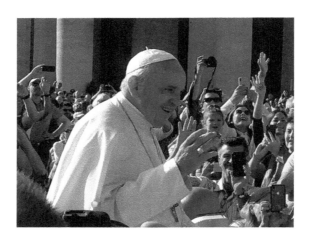

Rome 2019.

When do we start standing with Jesus, Rather than with the abusive "high priests"? When Do We Become Ashamed of Indifference and of being Bystanders?

In the Gospel of Mark, the arrest of Jesus is described in a very different and striking way within the synoptic gospels. Although we know it was Peter, Mark does not name the one who drew the sword and cut off the ear of the high priest's servant; he simply refers to him as *"one of the bystanders"* (Mark 14:47). As the account of Mark continues, they arrest Jesus, *"And they all left him and fled. Now a young man followed him wearing nothing but a linen cloth about his body. They seized him, but he left the cloth behind and ran off naked"* (Mark 14:51–52). **All** the "friends" and "followers" abandoned Jesus and fled. Peter, who happened to be Mark's "mentor" and is considered the "rock of our Church," was reduced in the Gospel to be solely a **"bystander."** Perhaps Mark was ashamed of how Peter responded; perhaps Mark was covering for or relating with his friend Peter—who knows. There are a lot of interpretations on the meaning of the young man who followed Jesus. One large belief is that the "young man" was Mark himself as one of the bystanders, **one of the mob** that followed the soldiers as they went after Jesus. The "linen cloth" is agreed by many to signify a "burial cloth" and to have "ran off naked" to signify **"shame."** So the young man who had been a follower of Jesus (vicariously through Peter and Paul) slipped away from the hold of those who hurt Jesus, and <u>ran away in shame</u>. Interpretations of Mark's account of everyone abandoning Jesus is of course more profound than this, but there is the strong interpretation that the young man <u>is ashamed for running away</u>.

Mark was not one of the disciples or apostles who spent time with Jesus, but they **were** his mentors and **one** of the apostles betrayed Jesus, **one** denied Him, and **all** of them deserted Jesus.

So if we **claim** to be Catholics, "Christian" disciples, and "followers" of Jesus:

WHEN, do **we** stop being solely "bystanders" as we witness and even promote and support our clericalist bishops and priests harming the Church and its members?

Do we stand up and object **only** when it is directed at our son, our daughter, a member of our immediate family, or someone who we are especially close to and love?

WHEN, do we stop believing that "ordination" automatically makes (human) men holy?

WHEN do we stop promoting and supporting clericalism, elitism, and the many clerical abuses?

Do we stand up and object **only** when it hits home or progresses to a major scandalous abuse as was in recent years exposed in our Church all over the world and as with Cardinal McCarrick?

Any "Catholic" who just stands by, keeps quiet, and turns away from repeated daily clerical abuses which is contrary to the teachings of Jesus or the cause of God, **should** be "ashamed"!

No "Christian" should ever be ashamed of our Catholic faith or of being "Catholics," but we **should** be ashamed of our clergy and of the perception that clergy of our Catholic Church give to those of different religions and be ashamed of the laity who merely stand by and keep quiet.

My parents were married at the cathedral, and my brothers and I "attended" mass there with them even before we were each born. We attended the adjoining Catholic grade school and served as altar boys at the cathedral before going on to the cathedral high school up the street. We would serve at mass before school at six thirty every morning. During the week, we would regularly be pulled out of class to serve at funerals which often included a comfortable limousine ride with the priest to the Catholic cemetery fifteen miles away. On weekends, we'd be asked to serve at any masses with the bishop or at weddings which often included tips the priest would forward from the groom. As grade-school altar boys, we benefited from the church clericalism, but it required a commitment and dedication on our part to serve as well as to our schoolwork, which we did with sincerity. We were taught at home, as most Catholics were in those days, about truly living our faith. We learned firsthand through our life-long experience and interaction with priests at church, at school, and at home, that we could and should be able to trust our priests. While many within the church were internally processing the transition to "Vatican II," our priests were not afraid to walk around the cathedral and school grounds and encounter parishioners and laity; they welcomed it. They were not always hiding as priests do now in their rectories or at their homes away from the church except for "select" parishioners.

Our mom and dad also taught us to be diligent, and to learn to follow our hearts in the decisions we make and who we trust. To my brothers and I, priests were simply men who ran the church who we treated with respect but who we were never in awe over or considered them as celebrities. We always had good instincts to know which priests and bishop(s) we should avoid being around as much as possible, especially those who might be too full of themselves or whose "behavior" depended on where they were or "who" was around. In those days, though, no one was walking around every day, including to church and school with cell phone cameras ready to post on Facebook. Praying and going to church was a little more "formal," and a lot more "personal and private," without the invasive social media. It appears to have become acceptable and expected for clergy to narcissistically post countless "selfies" and pictures taken of them, even during Mass during the consecration. They rate themselves by the number of Facebook "friends" they can generate. The priest "groupies" pretend or actually believe they are genuine "friends" within opportunistic "friendships" that are usually only in one direction and, most importantly, only "virtual."

> *"When you pray, do not be like the hypocrites, who love to stand and pray in the synagogues and on street corners so that others may see them"* (Matt. 6:5).

Jesus Himself, obviously very intentionally, warned us of "hypocrites." It is sad and unfortunate that our Catholic clergy always believe that Jesus was referring to "someone else." At a press conference to make a <u>political</u> statement, our bishop foolishly shouted "woe to you hypocrites" comparing politicians to the Scribes and Pharisees in the account of Matthew chapter 23.

It is an unfortunate reality that within our Church, none of us can ever know who we can really trust as sincere and authentic. Yet too many blindly and vulnerably trust the "collar."

It is also unfortunate that too many abuses of varying types and magnitudes within the church are continually covered up and swept under the rug. Sadly, if abuses progress to a point where lawsuits are filed, and quiet settlements are reached, everyone can pretend they never happened. Perhaps money makes victims shut up, and the abusers are allowed to continue their lives as exalted as ever, but it **does not** and **never** means that the abuse(s) never happened.

At our high school, run by the order of the De La Salle Brothers (also known as the "Christian Brothers"), the cafeteria was on the third floor with a rooftop courtyard enclosed by a chain-link fence. Students would gather there between and after lunch shifts. One afternoon after lunch, I was talking with a good friend from a prominent and well-respected family. Both our families were generational friends, and both families were very involved in the Church. He was a big guy in stature and had a big heart to match. He could <u>never</u> hurt anyone. As we looked over the wall, we saw the assistant principal, a Christian brother, walking down the alley below. I was caught off guard to see my friend pick up a trash can and, with both arms, hang it over the fence. Timing his stride up the alley with precision, he dropped the trash can three stories to crash on the ground behind the man. The Christian brother looked up to see who had dropped it but did not appear too startled, or perhaps he knew and preferred to avoid any confrontation and "exposure." I never found out why my friend did that; perhaps there was something deeper I don't know about. But I do know that I avoided being around the Christian brother and avoided any discussions with him any way I could. There was something creepy about him; there was something wrong with the attention he would give some of the guys.

Our class graduated that year and the following year that Christian brother became principal. In the coming years, lawsuits would confirm that my gut feelings had been correct and would expose that Christian brother. He had been accused of molesting boys in New Orleans and so he had been transferred to El Paso, where he was then accused of molesting additional guys at our high school. The dioceses settled with the families for about $4 million with about $1.6 million of that in the El Paso Diocese. I guess the "Church" knows money buys a different kind of "peace," and if the victims are paid off, everyone believes it all becomes okay; the harm inflicted is downplayed and all pretend it will "go away." In this case, as in many others, the "abuser" continued to be transferred and remained involved within the church (even around children) until he passed away with cancer in 2016. Lives, though, were affected and harmed.

The *York Daily Record* (YDR) published a complete listing of clergy who had been credibly accused of sexual abuse since 2018 in every diocese of every state in the United States and which YDR credits each of the names is available through the database maintained and published through the bishop accountability website. I was stunned by the staggering list…roughly 3,800 names…3,800 credibly accused members of the US clergy. With approximately thirty-eight thousand priests in the US, that would mean 10 percent or one in ten of all priests have been credibly accused of sexual abuse. How many victims are possibly afflicted? How many victims have suffered for the rest of their lives? Or even ended their lives? How many members of their families or friends became victims themselves sharing the pain and journeys with them? How many more victims were inflicted from abuses that were not of a sexual nature? Only God knows. The answer, whatever it may be, is a multiple factor of the number of abusive clergy. Staggering and saddening. **The wounds of <u>every</u> <u>single</u> <u>victim</u> fester for human lifetimes**. Despite what Church leaders believe and profess, it does **not** "just go away" with time. It is **not** just "the past" and that we should "just move on." **It <u>does not</u> just "go away." The wounds fester.**

The abuses have continued unchecked in our Church for almost two thousand years.

In the Letters of Augustine in the fourth century, Augustine wrote of a priest who was accused of raping a nun. Because there was no other information or witnesses other than the accusation of the nun, Bishop Augustine dismissed the accusation by saying it was the priest's word against the nun's. The priest was given the benefit of the doubt over the nun. From over the last two thousand years of history of the Church, we know that <u>either</u> the priest <u>or</u> the nun was telling the truth, but we know also, with certainty, that <u>either</u> one of them, regardless of Holy Orders, was possibly capable of <u>not</u> telling the truth. We will never know the truth in this one incident out of many that would come through the ages, but one can only imagine what happened, in those days, at that time in history, to that one woman (and her family), who happened to be a nun, at the bottom ranks of the Church religious hierarchy.

Pope Francis has with wisdom and against much opposition, been standing up for the powerful roles of women in the Church, even to elevating St. Mary Magdalene's deserving place in history. A truly loving disciple who was demonized by the Church but always understood and supported the ministry of Jesus and never betrayed or abandoned Him or ran away. In June of 2016, Pope Francis issued a decree to elevate Mary Magdalene's memorial to a feast day in the Church of the same level with the apostles. On the July 22, 2016, feast, our local diocese for the most part ignored the decree. When I asked a priest why the feast was not honored, I was told the diocese (bishop) was not promoting the Feast of Mary Magdalene. At the cathedral, alternate readings were used in the Mass liturgy. Throughout the world Church, women continue to be discriminated, hurt, taken for granted, and taken advantage of; some have even been excommunicated in the past for believing that their relationship with God and their ability to teach and nurture loving Christians might be on equal (or even higher) levels to their male counterparts. Through the ages women have been pillars of our churches and have been grossly taken for granted and abused every day and in many ways which they are not even aware of. Many overpiously deny or refuse to acknowledge abuses they continue to endure or witness.

The clergy "physical" abuses over the ages, however, never began with each of their first sexual abuse victims. For each individual priest, it began with clericalism, elitism, the abuse of clerical position and authority, the belief that they are "untouchable," and the lack of accountability that at some point occurs in every neighborhood church in every diocese of every city of the United States. Little by little, the acknowledgment of receipt of and the gratitude for gifts and favors lovingly given to them diminishes; clergy begin to expect and demand them, and it becomes second nature. Some members of the laity generously donate money and time, and participate at church, <u>more for the priest and for their access to him</u>. Unfortunately, wealth and prominence in the community also gains one greater access to the clergy. But every single privilege clergy are given every meal that is opportunistically "<u>expected</u>" to be paid by the parishioner, every dollar bill placed in their hands walking out of a mass, every rude behavior we witness and keep our silence to and fail to expect an apology and accountability, potentially supports and fuels the next level of abusive behavior.

The impact a father's example has on his sons is beyond measure. The bishop of a diocese is called to be that "father" and example to the priests under his care. Diocesan clergy, without the love, support, and guidance of an authentic and caring bishop, is identical to children without the nurturing love and guidance of their parents.

The YDR article states, "Bishops say the names [on the list of credibly accused clergy] represent sins of the past and a church that's moving forward in transparency." However, "transparency" has little meaning without remorse, accountability, and truly reaching toward the healing of individuals. Their responsibility rests far from just saying, "Let's pray for them" and leaving it to divine intervention by saying the victims are "in God's hands," and that priests are "men of God."

Yet in our human weaknesses, we support and promote clergy abuses in even very simple ways.

After Sunday Mass one morning, one of the young, recently ordained priests asked to join us for breakfast. It was, of course, a very pleasant Sunday morning. After the meal, the priest stood up and said he needed to leave. He walked out of the restaurant, taking it for granted without any word or gesture that the cost of breakfast was covered. It was understood. Of course it was, without question, and with great pleasure on our part. But at such an early point, only weeks in his priesthood, having meals paid for was already something to be expected and taken for granted. Years later, the "expected" free meals have continued with laity throughout the diocese, but now at more exclusive and expensive restaurants, and at restaurants all over the world on "pilgrimage" vacations, <u>all taken for granted and expected</u>. I was once told (by a priest) that the older priest(s) would tell the young priests, "Let the people pay. They can afford it!"

In instances with other "religious" order priests, however, there were occasions where the priest almost argued to pay for the meal. In one instance, a humble priest grabbed the side of my arm and said, "Please! My turn, allow me to buy <u>your</u> meal. I appreciate everything you do." As much as I personally struggle with allowing any priest to pay for meals, the gesture and gratitude is beyond any heartfelt expression, including simple meals with the priest at church. Knowing that meals are not always expected, taken for granted, or even almost demanded, they becomes a joyful and meaningful "family" occasion. A meal becomes a true gathering of "breaking bread." In every aspect of our lives, love has to be both given and received with arms open.

One evening, while attending a diocesan dinner, two of our "higher-ranking" members of clergy joined our table where several couples were seated. The handful of priests who even showed up that evening for the gathering were obviously there to be seen by the bishop and to get their free meal and wine. After the meal was served, the two priests began engaging discussion between themselves of their own personal interests. Their language, though, was that which most loving people would never use amongst friends or at their dinner table, using the F-word and even the "G...D" expression. It was almost as if they were trying to see who at the table they could shock or perhaps hoping someone might think *Hey, these guys are "cool" being regular guys*. But NO, personally, I was disgusted especially for the women sitting at our table. Many of the people at the dinner are conservative, who believe priests walk on water. Since the dinner was being hosted by the bishop and I did not want to embarrass any one at the table, squeezing my hands under the table, I used God's two gifts of free will and restraint to keep my mouth shut.

To this day, though, I deeply regret not asking them politely to have respect not just for the women, but everyone at the table and the adjacent tables. As the two proud priests sat back and continued cussing, everyone's wine glasses were empty. The younger priest got up, got a bottle of wine from the open bar, and served the older priest and himself. He offered or served no one else at the table with an arrogant gesture that implied that in his eyes, someone at the table was "supposed" to have served the priests. As "priests" and the "hosts" of the dinner, though, they should have been walking around serving the tables. As guests began to leave, the priest went, grabbed a bottle of wine from the bar for himself, and left. Abusive. And the failure of the "ministry" purpose of the dinner was quite "obvious."

Our priests are given very comfortable housing that are much more than just "modest" homes. Our US bishops are allowed excessive, often magnificent homes. Our local bishop is provided a large four-bedroom home. How can "extravagance and excess" ever promote humbleness? Should it be considered okay and appropriate for bishops to opportunistically and secretly, without public disclosure, move any member(s) of his family into diocesan homes which are intended for our priests? Does the lack of transparency and to attempting to be under the radar, imply a knowledge or sense of abusiveness? Why is lack of transparency so prevalent by our clergy?

Every year, the Foundation for the Diocese of El Paso hosts a fundraiser dinner and raffle. Diocesan clergy, who will not make the effort or time to spend with average parishioners, are auctioned off for thousands of dollars to the highest bidder, for exclusive private dinners or for a round of golf with the golfing priest(s). Priests are obligated by Canon Law to try to be available to everyone alike without giving preference. <u>Spending time with a priest should never be at a price or to the highest bidder</u>. The entire concept of raffling off priests as celebrities is horrible in itself. It even promotes jealousy between them when one fetches a larger bid than the other. For the bishop, diocese, and anyone who might care, it is easy to keep track of which member(s) of the clergy generate the most revenue for the diocese or has the biggest following of "fans," which has absolutely nothing to do with spiritual inspiration. And usually, and sadly, both the priest and highest bidder gloat with "pride."

Also <u>every</u> single year and sometimes twice a year, the bishop's new rector would travel on world vacations which the church prefers to refer to as "pilgrimages." He was very obviously an example, promoter, and envy amongst other priests. In the "Rio Grande Catholic," a newspaper published monthly by the El Paso Diocese, advertisements are published for travel with a priest, sometimes sadly, with two priests per trip. For "pilgrimages" a surcharge is normally added to the cost of the individuals traveling, and a minimum number of travelers is required, to pay for the costs of the priest(s). Based on those advertisements, during the first years of our new bishop between 2016 and 2019, and with only one of the travel agents (member of the parish) the same five to six diocesan priests traveled every single year (without rotating all priests in the diocese). Based on the published travel prices, the total value of travel received by that one group of priests was approximately $110,293. Above and beyond regular vacations, time off, and time to plan and prepare for the trips, the group of priests were away from their parishes (in some cases, churches were left without any parish priest) for approximately 6648 "priest" hours (277 priest days).

During the 2020 COVID pandemic, travel was, of course, banned and interrupted, but the same six diocesan priests had all previously scheduled trips to **Germany** to attend a theatrical performance of the Lord's Passion, with an "advertised" combined value of $31,041 and 1,344 hours (fifty-six "priest" days) planned to be away from their parishes. In the April 2021 issue of the *Rio Grande Catholic*, travel to Germany for the performance by two of the same six members of the clergy was already being advertised three months before the bishop announced plans to reopen the churches on July 1, 2021. In spring of 2022, "vacations" for 2023 were already being planned and published.

I know that I myself hope to one day visit and vacation in Germany, but there is something very wrong in pretending that the Oberammergau Passion play in Germany is a religious "pilgrimage." For centuries, the Germany presentation has been the source of deep controversy for anti-Semitism. The play has been described as an artistic presentation more than it is a religious one. Hitler is said to have attended and supported the performance, which for centuries portrayed Jesus being crucified and killed by ALL the Jewish people. The performance has been believed for many years to actually have played a part in the persecution and killing of millions of Jews during the Holocaust. Jesus was a Jew who was **not** killed by **all** the Jews but rather by the Pharisees and high priests. The fact that the play continued for many years, contrary to the "*Nostra Aetate*" document of Vatican II, which repudiated years of Christian teaching, is a major issue that should concern Catholics and Christians. The presentation should not be avoided, but rather be recognized as an opportunity to be promoted as an educational process to Catholics and not as an excuse for abusive vacation travel for clergy and their lack of pastoral care.

With the Oberammergau passion play as well as all the abusive clergy "pilgrimage" vacations, it is good that we, as Catholics believe in the ascension and resurrection and don't have to worry about Jesus turning in His grave.

Sure, members of the clergy need to get away and deserve occasional travel on a true "pilgrimage." However, every single year is abusive. Also abusive and selfish is not rotating the opportunity to travel to all priests of the diocese rather than only to the same few priests every single year because they have a guaranteed "celebrity" following. What a loss of an opportunity to invite a less-fortunate member of the parish who could never afford a trip of a lifetime and truly inspiring "pilgrimage" for them. The most unfortunate part, though, is that the costs of the trips which are fully paid for by others, are "expected" and taken for granted, by a majority if not all of the priests. Clergy living comfortably the lifestyles of the rich and famous is definitely not religiously attractive. When trying to make the travel quotas, they will often tell parishioners, "You should come, you should come!" without realization and consideration of the fact that the average parishioner needs to budget that extravagant world travel time and expenses, sometimes with difficulty and having to sacrifice other life priorities; and definitely not for planning travel every single year. World travel is addictive; it is easy for financially comfortable members of the laity to embrace and support the travel in order to spend private time with and become "friends" with priests. But it promotes abuse, and usually after their first experience, the extravagance, costs, and abusive nature of the trip(s) mean little to the priests, and very addictive for abuse.

Sadly, even after receiving a free "vacation," our clergy do not share the experiences with the church "family" community, even as religiously inspirational and educational tools. When our young priest was asked (unfortunately not by a more affluent member of the church) to share his photos and experiences (hoping for clerical insight), he rudely responded to go ask one of the others who went on the trip. The "pilgrimage" vacations in our diocese are only for the personal selfish satisfaction of our priests. If one was to look, would we find that the words "overindulgence," "abstinence," "temperance," "restraint," "moderation," "self-control," and others in the documents and canons of our Church? We can be sure we will not find them in the vocabulary of many diocesan clergy unless they are judging members of the laity.

Since our new bishop arrived to our diocese, the majority of our priests and future seminarians have been recruited and imported from other less fortunate countries. Increasing priest counts in any diocese is a feather in the mitre of any bishop to the Vatican. Even after Archbishop McCarrick had already been credibly accused, he took the opportunity to brag to Pope John Paul of ordaining a group of priests on Pope John's birthday; he was reported to have responded, "*Today was a good day.*" In our diocese, it is far easier to increase clergy "counts" by importing priests from underprivileged conditions than admitting failure to inspire vocations from within our own community and families. But rather than inspiring vocations from within our local families, our bishop and clergy through the example of their lives actually disillusion and discourage members of our church. Perhaps there are multiple reasons why our bishop maintains a close relationship with the Mexican bishops across our border.

But to <u>pretend</u> that "inspiration" is the driving force of any increases in clergy "count" is deceiving and unfortunate. In the US, a priest imported from a less fortunate country can be guaranteed a better life, but <u>not</u> necessarily a better life lived as a "priest." At the end of the day, it is the priest himself who is often abandoned for costs and sacrifices that come with travel and visa applications. Perhaps if these imported priests come to realize how they are being exploited and abused themselves, maybe one day they will become better priests.

Pope Francis has specifically warned and directed against assigning priests as administrators rather than pastors and if necessary, <u>only with exceptions and for very limited time frames</u>. In June 2020, within his "Instruction for 'The pastoral conversion of the Parish community in the service of the evangelizing mission of the Church, of the Congregation for the Clergy," it states:

> *Section VIII.b. Parish Administrator;*
>
> *75. If it is not possible to proceed immediately with the appointment of the Parish Priest, the appointment of Parish Administrators[107] must be done only in conformity with what is established in the canonical norms[108]. In effect, the office is essentially transitory and is exercised while awaiting the appointment of the new Parish Priest. For this reason,* **_it is illegitimate_** *for the diocesan Bishop to appoint a Parish Administrator and to leave him in that position for an extended period of time, more than a year, or even permanently, in order to avoid the appointment of a Parish Priest. <u>As experience shows,</u>* **_<u>this solution is often adopted in order to circumvent the requirements of the law</u>_** <u>*regarding the principle of stability for the Parish Priest, which constitutes a violation, with harm to both the mission of the priest and that of the community itself.*</u> *Because of the uncertainty about the presence of a pastor, the Parish is not able to program*

*far-reaching evangelization plans and must limit its
pastoral care to mere preservation.*

As of July 1, 2021, the El Paso Diocese was approaching almost
50 percent of its parishes with administrators rather than pastors and
appointing administrators for lengthy, extended periods. Perhaps it is
indicative of the inability of our bishop to properly assign and manage
priests in our parishes. Perhaps the bishop feels he has more authority
over them as administrators rather than as pastors. Whatever the reason, it is obviously contrary to the directives and messages of Francis
to clergy, and to the Motu Propios (decrees issued by the pontiff for
reasons he considers sufficient and important), which he has issued.

On September 30, 2019, Pope Francis issued a Motu Propio
with his apostolic letter "Aperuit Illis," through which instituted
"Sunday of the Word of God" to now be celebrated every year by the
entire Church on the Third Sunday of Ordinary Time. On January
26, 2020, on its first celebration, Francis in his homily took the perspective of going "to the root of [Jesus's] preaching, to the very source
of the word of life." **The apostolic letter was <u>profound,</u> describing
in detail its major significance, <u>even toward advancing Vatican II</u>.**
During those same days in January, our bishop was <u>required</u> to report
to Rome for his Ad Lumina report to Francis while he and our diocese disregarded the entire purpose of the Motu Propio, failing to see
Francis's intention; and failing in the major opportunity to inspire
evangelization and spiritual growth in the diocese.

That Sunday of the Word of God was the day after the Feast
of the Conversion of St. Paul. St. Paul's temporary blindness during
his conversion has been said to symbolize religious blindness. It is

religious blindness where our abusive clergy within the Institution of our Church shine their light and fail us.

Disregard of papal directives is, in itself, a form of clerical abuse.

For the Ad Limina visit, every five years, the bishop of every diocese in the world is <u>required</u> in accordance to Canon Law (Canon 399) to submit a report to the pontiff on the state of his particular diocese. Since the reports are private, we can only imagine the many impressive acts and "milestones" are misrepresented within our particular diocese. Also in accordance to Canon Law, sometime during the same year of the status report, every bishop is <u>required</u> to report to Rome to <u>venerate</u> the tombs of Peter and Paul (Canon 400). For centuries, our bishops have been required to venerate the "royalty" and holiness of past "bishops" rather than to the Holy Land of the birth, life, death, and resurrection of Jesus Christ. During the same required visit to Rome, the bishop(s) are required to also report to the pontiff for their "Ad Limina" visit (Canon 400). The visit(s) with the pontiff, are <u>required</u> by Canon Law and have absolutely <u>nothing</u> to do with the bishop's relationship, support, or friendship with the pope as has been implied or published in our diocesan news. The ad limina visits demonstrate how clericalism is promoted in very simple ways to satisfy outdated and very fallible Church canons and laws.

God blessed my life to have met, come to know, admire, and cherish a bishop from another diocese. During his Ad Limina visit, he sent daily video reports to his entire diocese on what he did and experienced, who he met with and why, etc. and explained the significances. Before retiring to bed <u>every evening</u>, he would lead his diocese in gentle prayer (via video). The bishop lovingly and humbly included his diocese in his statutory visit to Rome rather than attempting to arrogantly impress and artificially represent his visit as a special "papal" connection to "Rome," as others do. It clearly demonstrates where a bishop's heart is (or isn't). This bishop has an inner peace that can only come from the awareness that he can only be a reflection of God's light, not a source of it. He continues to be a positive down-to-earth example and hope for our Church (and for me). Whether or not he fully comprehends the depth of my gratitude both personally and as a Catholic, I continue to admire how he handles his position in the hierarchy, and he continues regularly in my heartfelt prayers.

In contrast to church leaders within our particular diocese, names are not important unless personal help or donations are needed. They divide rather than unite members throughout the diocese and indifferently dismiss members who stop attending church or leave altogether. The "sheep" are separated as if to be of different "colors." Members of the laity who object to wrongs of the church are chastised with the sarcastic attitude *"if anyone is unhappy and leaves the Church, don't worry, they'll be back!"* But many of the "sheep" will NOT "be back" and in fact may become better Christians and even better "Catholics," away from the Catholic diocesan clergy and physical church buildings, rather than to being mere "followers" and "bystanders." They soon hopefully realize that being compared and referred to as "SHEEP" is by no means a "compliment." And a shepherd who does not care for his sheep will eventually lose his flock. A "lost" shepherd can only lead sheep through the "wide" gate and to the wolves.

The Parable of the Lost Shepherd

At mass one morning, the Gospel was "*The Parable of the Lost Sheep*" (Luke 15:4–7). In his homily, our young priest said that in today's current times, if one of the sheep were to stray, it would become "*barbacoa.*" Barbacoa is a traditional Mexican barbecue. His direction in his homily had a serious thought process, but he also thought he was being cute, and the parishioners laughed, but unfortunately, it is in fact the current day position of our local diocesan priests. If one of the flock stops attending or leaves the church, complains, or stands up to wrongs in the church, they are in fact tied, placed on their personal altar, sacrificed and "cooked" and become "barbacoa," rather than (if clergy even care at all) the "shepherd" removing his collar, rolling up his sleeves, fixing the fence he broke, helping to balm and heal any wounds, and then rejoicing.

For years, I was one of the sheep in the herd where the diocesan bishop and clergy pretended to be shepherds caring for the sheep. Until one day, the break in the fence was so large I could see clearly through it. I didn't care for all the thorny weeds in the ill kept pen and wandered out to search for nourishing green grass to chew on in the warm light of the sun, and wide-open mountains to climb toward the clear blue skies. But as you turn and look back with a better view and without the dark shadows, you see that behind the broken fence that set you free, the entire house and barn are broken, and that the shepherds are actually wolves wearing masks with "priest collars," merely fattening up the sheep for their own glory and feast. Very few of the sheep ever look toward the narrow gate opening, and most of the sheep are exactly what Bernard Lonergan, the Jesuit theologian, defined as "drifters"…mere followers who take the easy path and never question or search for (Sacratic) **truth**. They get "led" to shearers to be shorn, or to the slaughter house. The sheep are not even aware, care, or know that they <u>should</u> care.

The role of the shepherd is an important one for those who need or prefer to be "led" and to be "told" where to go and what is "right or wrong" and **<u>trusting</u>** that they're right. The sheep would be surprised to see, though, that the "narrow gate," from where one can hear the voice of (Jesus) (John 10:27), the true shepherd is right beyond the "shadows" being cast by the "wolf" (priest), who lead them through the wider gate. But the "priest's" gate and path lead meek and scared "sheep" running off somewhere to hide and get away to "Emmaus" rather than to "Galilee."

I use the homily of our young priest to describe a different but realistic twist to the *"Parable of the Lost Sheep."* That which the one who repents is the shepherd who actually caused the sheep to leave in the first place. The sheep wandered off <u>to get away from the abuse, from being spiritually starved and misled</u> and ultimately find truth through the "narrow gate." The "voice" they had always recognized of the abusive shepherd <u>is what they run away from, not go toward</u>. **It is not the sheep that are lost but the shepherd**, and <u>after the shepherd repents</u>, he then leads the herd to green grass, feeds the sheep and cares for them; and it is <u>then</u> that they follow his voice. This version of the parable is realistic, but **the repentant shepherds are only in our "prayers."**

Our diocese is thirsty for leadership, inspiration, and "parresia," and to being "relentless" in faith. I will never claim to personally know what the millions of horrific church sex abuse victims have gone through over the centuries and throughout the world, but I have had a glimpse of what any victim of any level of abuse by clergy of the church has to endure within the church, a glimpse that has inflicted great harm. All repeated clerical abuses, no matter the form or magnitude, are damaging to our entire Church and are contrary toward the mission of Christ.

Our Catholic clergy take a vow for the cause of God when they are ordained and voluntarily give up their right to have intimate relationships in a Church that does not allow priests to marry and have children and families. At times, it must stir an intense burning restlessness within them. A restlessness that St. Augustine described as *"You have made us for yourself, O Lord, and our heart is restless until it rests in you."* But this implies the cause of God is intended.

Whether or not taking those vows are a true calling, "religion" is what "clergy" choose to study and choose to do for a living. They are <u>obligated</u> by Canon Law and by their vows and (hopefully) called to strive to be holy in humbleness. They should **want** to strive for that. We <u>should be able</u> to hold them to higher standards and they <u>should be expected</u> to be held to higher standards. To reach for and be held to those higher standards should also further humble them in their relationship with God.

<u>Being held to higher standards is the whole crux of ordination and priesthood! It is what allows a priest to be an "example"!</u>

35

The example that shows, or should show, that he has come to know Jesus.

When Jorge Bergoglio became Pope Francis, he used a wonderful term "*parresia*" while talking to the conclave. This awesome word is derived from the Greek word *parrhesia*, which implies to be bold in speaking out, not necessarily in the right to speak, but in our moral obligation to speak the truth for the common good regardless of the personal risk there might be.

A "bold" religious order priest, introduced a few of us to the life changing works of Bernard Lonergan, the Jesuit priest and theologian who lived his life studying <u>our obligation as people of faith to constantly search for the truth through the transcendental precepts of being "attentive" in experience, being "intelligent" in understanding, being "reasonable" in judgment, being "responsible" in decisions, and in all our authenticity to "being in love"</u>. We learn through the works of giants on whose shoulders we stand as sources of wisdom, truth, understanding and knowing. It is one reason that Raphael's fresco titled "School of Athens" regarding "rational truth" at the Vatican is so impressive. The philosopher Socrates is only one example of those giants, and one who was sentenced to death for his use of "parresia," to going against common opinions, refusing to worship the "gods" of Athens, and accused of corrupting student youth in their search for truth. Our search for truth leads us, and can <u>only</u> lead us, to the Father, the Son and the Holy Spirit.

Being true "Catholics" is not for the weak or for sheep that simply follow others through the widest path and gate. Being true "Catholics" requires strength of our belief and faith in Jesus, to follow Jesus, for the cause of God. Jesus Himself enlightens and lets us know what the cause of God is if we listen to the Holy Spirit and listen to God's heartbeat. We should never be surprised, or frightened, if we find ourselves enlightened to teachings of Jesus that, just might be contrary to the teachings and example of our abusive Catholic clergy.

The deeper we fall in love with God, the more our hearts soften and we become loving, trusting, and vulnerable. Loving and trusting people of faith are very forgiving to those who "know not what they do" or who do and are remorseful; and only the weak hearted turn their heads and look the other way to repeated abuses and infliction of harm within a Church that continues to thrive in secrecy and the lack of transparency.

How do Catholics, though, who have been so hurt, disenchanted, and no longer find <u>credible</u> "shepherd" priests in their parish, their community, or their diocese, continue as "Catholics"?

Short of abandoning the Church one loves, what does one do?

Where does one go?

Let us first remember where we came from…

Where did we come from?

Every year as Lent gives way to Easter, we hear the beautiful account of Creation from Genesis. We hear the words, but sometimes, we even listen and take it to heart. It should be humbling.

> ### The Beginning
> *In the beginning God created the heavens and the earth. Now the earth was formless and empty, darkness was over the surface of the deep, and the Spirit of God was hovering over the waters. And God said, "Let there be light," and there was light. God saw that the light was good, and he separated the light from the darkness. God called the light "day," and the darkness he called "night." And there was evening, and there was morning.*
>
> ### The First Day.
> *And God said, "Let there be a vault between the waters to separate water from water." So God made the vault and separated the water under the vault from the water above it. And it was so. God called the vault "sky." And there was evening, and there was morning.*

The Second Day.

And God said, "Let the water under the sky be gathered to one place, and let dry ground appear." And it was so. God called the dry ground "land," and the gathered waters he called "seas." And God saw that it was good. Then God said, "Let the land produce vegetation: seed-bearing plants and trees on the land that bear fruit with seed in it, according to their various kinds." And it was so. The land produced vegetation: plants bearing seed according to their kinds and trees bearing fruit with seed in it according to their kinds. And God saw that it was good. And there was evening, and there was morning.

The Third Day.

And God said, "Let there be lights in the vault of the sky to separate the day from the night, and let them serve as signs to mark sacred times, and days and years, and let them be lights in the vault of the sky to give light on the earth." And it was so. God made two great lights—the greater light to govern the day and the lesser light to govern the night. He also made the stars. God set them in the vault of the sky to give light on the earth, to govern the day and the night, and to separate light from darkness. And God saw that it was good. And there was evening, and there was morning.

The Fourth Day.

And God said, "Let the water teem with living creatures, and let birds fly above the earth across the vault of the sky." So God created the great creatures of the sea and every living thing with which the water teems and that moves about in it, according to their kinds, and every winged bird according to its kind. And God saw that it was good. God blessed them and said, "Be fruitful and increase in number and fill the water in the seas, and let the birds increase on the earth." And there was evening, and there was morning.

The Fifth Day.

And God said, "Let the land produce living creatures according to their kinds: the livestock, the creatures that move along the ground, and the wild animals, each according to its kind." And it was so. God made the wild animals according to their kinds, the livestock according to their kinds, and all the creatures that move along the ground according to their kinds. And God saw that it was good.

Then God said, "Let us make mankind in our image, in our likeness, so that they may rule over the fish in the sea and the birds in the sky, over the livestock and all the wild animals,[a] and over all the creatures that move along the ground." (Gen. 1:1–26)

NOTE: Let us keep in mind that in Genesis, *"Let **us** make mankind in **our** image, in **our** likeness."* In the very first book of the Bible, God is referred to in plural sense. **The Holy Trinity**.

THE STORY OF THE NATIONS
The Garden of Eden

This is the account of the heavens and the earth when they were created, when the Lord God made the earth and the heavens. Now no shrub had yet appeared on the earth and no plant had yet sprung up, for the Lord God had not sent rain on the earth and there was no one to work the ground, but streams came up from the earth and watered the whole surface of the ground. (**Gen. 21:4–6**)

Then the Lord God formed a man from the dust of the ground and breathed into his nostrils the breath of life, and the man became a living being. (Gen. 21:7)

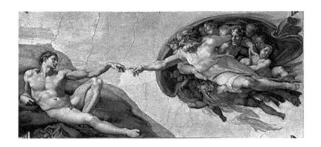

Universally available image of "The Creation of Adam" by
Michelangelo (1508–1512), Sistine Chapel, Rome.

There is profound belief that Michelangelo portrayed God's red
cloak in the shape of the human brain to signify the endowment of
man with intelligence. Man is depicted already alive, fully grown,
with his eyes wide open. The fingers of God and man are reaching, but not touching, to signify "transmission" of intelligence and of
love, through God's energy frequency.

> **So God created mankind in his own
> image, in the image of God he created them;**
> *male and female he created them. God blessed them
> and said to them, "Be fruitful and increase in num-
> ber; fill the earth and subdue it. Rule over the fish in
> the sea and the birds in the sky and over every living
> creature that moves on the ground." Then God said,
> "I give you every seed-bearing plant on the face of
> the whole earth and every tree that has fruit with
> seed in it. <u>They will be yours for food.</u> And to all the
> beasts of the earth and all the birds in the sky and all*

the creatures that move along the ground—every-thing that has the breath of life in it—I give every green plant for food."

And it was so. **God saw all that he had made, and it was very good.**

And there was evening, and there was morning. ***The Sixth Day.*** (Gen. 1:27–31)

The Seventh Day Followed

Thus the heaven and the earth and all their array were completed… God blessed the seventh day and made it **holy***, because on it He rested from all the work He had done in creation.* (**Gen. 2:1–3**)

But that is not the end of the "story."

It is a "living" story.

Creation by God continues between every instant moment in time.

With every rotation of the planets around the sun;

With every sunrise and sunset.

With every newborn child and every death of a loved one.

With every seed planted and every tree that falls and returns to the earth;

With every act of kindness and love we give expecting nothing in return;

With every night that turns to day

With every second of every day, of every year, for eternity.

"Creation" and "love," beyond our earthly imaginings continues.

By and through God and no one else, but God

> *"God's seed is in us. If it were tended by a good, wise and industrious laborer, it would then flourish all the better, and would grow up to God, whose seed it is, and its fruits would be like God's own nature. The seed of a pear tree grows into a pear tree, the seed of a nut tree grows to be a nut tree, the seed of God grows to be God"* (Meister Eckhart 1260–1328).

Keeping in mind where we come from as well as all of God's blessings, should humble each and every one of us, inspired to aspire to live holy, loving lives in what was meant to be an extremely blessed, holy, loving and compassionate world.

There is a caveat, a caution we need all to keep in mind to the "Garden of Eden": the beautiful paradise with perfect climate given to man where all we could possibly ask for was there for our "<u>taking.</u>" <u>Adam and Eve ABUSED the gift!</u> And man was expelled from the garden to a **life of toil**; and man reproduced and filled the earth with lawlessness and even greater **abuses**. So except for Noah and his family who were in good favor, the world was destroyed and cleaned by the cataclysmic flood. After many months in the ark, the families went out onto the new earth. And God said, ***"Never again... since the <u>desires</u> of the human heart are evil from youth"*** and from then on. *"All the days of the earth, seedtime and harvest, cold and heat. Summer and winter, and day and night shall not cease"* (Gen. 8:21–22).

Humans <u>now</u> had to work for their food, and their life spans were reduced.

And God's gift of free will to man, to choose between right or wrong, continued.

Man again began to multiply and fill the earth; and the ancestors of Abraham began. But with the "evil" in the DESIRES of man, ABUSE since the beginning of man, **coveting** from the abundant **blessings and gifts from God** with our **gift of free will** has <u>continued to cause harm</u>.

All God has ever asked from us is to tell/show others about His love and to love one another.

There is no biblical account of any promise of life without pain other than eternal life. But perhaps it is true that real love can be experienced only after having experienced deep pain; and that we must have really loved someone, sometime in our life, and know what love truly is, in order to feel the pain of others, to avoid causing pain, and to desire to help anyone, in pain.

The more we love, the less likely we are to hurt others and the more capacity we have to love and to feel and absorb the pain of others, and <u>walk</u> with them.

Jesus showed us this through His Crucifixion for all mankind.

> *"I have found the paradox that if I love until it hurts, then there is no hurt only more love"* (Mother Teresa).

So what happens to good men who choose to become "priests" and who profess to dedicate their lives to the service of God, for the cause of God, and then with the gift of their free, will allow the "evil" in the DESIRES of their human hearts to grow?

Does ordination into the self-referential fraternity of Catholic "priests" <u>facilitate</u> the deterioration in hearts of otherwise good men; the destruction of their capacity for humbleness, compassion, and love; and their fall into their abusive lifestyles?

As "Christians," what becomes of their belief in: **Jesus**, the <u>life</u> of Jesus, the <u>teachings</u> of Jesus?

What is it, that <u>all</u> of us as "**Christians**" believe in?

What do we believe In?

Trinitarian "Love": The Father, the Son, and the Holy Spirit
Is It Necessary to Announce the Holy Spirit to Receive its Love?

Then the eleven disciples went to Galilee, to the mountain where Jesus had told them to go. When they saw him, they worshiped him; but some doubted. Then Jesus came to them and said, "All authority in heaven and on earth has been given to me. Therefore go and make disciples of all nations, baptizing them in the name of

The Father and of the Son
and of the Holy Spirit,

and teaching them to obey everything I have commanded you. And surely I am with you always, to the very end of the age. (Matt. 28:16–20)

Painting depicting the Holy Trinity by Guido Reni (1625) above the
Altar of the Santissima Trinita dei Pellegrine Church in Rome.

A central affirmation of Catholics and most Christians is the doctrine of the Trinity. The wonderful absolute mystery of the Holy
Trinity fills our divine souls and human hearts with the unity of the
Father, Son, and Holy Spirit as three persons in one God. All three,
are the one and the same omnipotent love in perfect authenticity. In
contrast, humans, as seen in some of our clergy, might be three different people in one person, depending on where they are, who they're

with, and how many cameras are focused on them; disingenuous lack of authenticity.

But in our Catholic, Christian faith, God through His Son, became man, Jesus, fully human, so that with the Holy Spirit, we may come to know our Father God divinely.

As "believing" Catholics, what is this power, this divine "energy" field, this highest form of energy in all creation that makes the "Father" and "Son" and "Holy Spirit" as "one"? That makes God present whenever two or more are gathered in His name? That gathered all the apostles and Mary, in His name after the resurrection *"all devoted...to one accord to prayer"* (Acts 1:14). That *"came from the sky...like a strong driving wind"* (Acts 2:2)? What is that energy in our souls that comes with us when we are created, keeps us attached to God during our lives on earth, and then takes us back to God's embrace when we die?

It is the highest and only form of energy in which God exists = "LOVE."

All four canonical gospels describe the baptism of Jesus, as the sky opening and the Holy Spirit descending on Him in the form of a dove. The "Father" was sending His love in the "Holy Spirit" to His "Beloved Son." God the "Father" was communicating with His "Son" with the "Holy Spirit" via the greatest state of energy that exists: love.

Genesis tells us that we were created in the image of all three: the Father, Son, and Holy Spirit. Quantum physics tells us that we, as human beings, are energy fields of atoms manifested and held together in the form of physical bodies. There is extreme profundity in that.

In quantum physics exists the fascinating phenomenon known as "quantum entanglement" where microscopically two particles of matter when in the same state, no longer exist as separate particles but together as one, even when separated by distance. When the energy fields of two individual human beings resonate, harmonize, and coalesce is when we "fall in love" with each other. When truly in "love," and the energy fields are resonating physically, spiritually, and emotionally, love then unites the two who then exist united regardless of distance. It is the same phenomenon between a mother and her children, between siblings, between best friends, between anyone who truly believes in the teachings of Jesus and God's greatest commandment.

This connection of powerful love energy is what gives us a "sixth sense" or a "premonition" with another human being. It is how we feel another's mutual love for us, what connects a mother to her children, and to know when something is wrong even if apart at different ends of the earth. It is what makes prayer together in groups so powerful; in the only language and energy that God exists, "love energy." It is what makes two or more gathered in agreement and in His Name and love so powerful. It is how souls communicate and what unites us **with GOD** in the Eucharist.

A few years ago, a group of about forty of us were preparing for a retreat. While we were in formation, one of the participants was blessed with the birth of his grandson, but premature and being gravely rushed into surgery. I wrote a prayer and sent it via text message to the group, asking that at 7:00 p.m. that evening we all stop what we're doing and pray the same words together. I really wasn't expecting responses, but immediately at 7:00 p.m., my phone began tinging: *te-ting*, *te-ting*, *te-ting*, forty or so times, with an "Amen" attached to each *te-ting*. Within those few seconds of *tings*, my hand which was holding the phone began trembling uncontrollably. As I reached to hold my phone with both hands, I felt an energy go down my arm into my chest. Perhaps it was the phone overloaded from all the responses coming in at the same time, only God knows. But I definitely felt the power of prayer with two or more gathered in God's name, and some form of "energy" field uniting forty or so men, in a way which I had never imagined.

"And God said, 'Let there be LIGHT and there was light'" (Gen. 1:3). God's power, love, and grace are referred to as "the Light of God." In physics, the quantity of energy that would be required to travel faster than light would be unimaginable. To even try to understand the energy frequency and the power of God's love and light is humanly impossible as is also trying to understand or control the unlimited volume that God "pours" on us. Our clergy try to convince the open arms and hearts of Catholic Christians that they control the gate valves to that love, the light switches to that light, and when, where, how much, or how often anyone can receive.

Being true "Christians," regardless what religion we practice, is powerful, but **never** ever power "giving" to any human to control **what is of and from God.**

The LOVE of the Holy Trinity; of God...the Father, the Son, and the Holy Spirit, is not solely a belief of Trinitarian Christians and "Catholics," it is a real and actual "existence." The "presence" of

God's love, light, and energy field in our lives is not merely an "idea" that we "believe" in; it is a very tangible part of our everyday lives.

The love and power of God, the Father, Son, and the Holy Spirit is part of the mission of Jesus that the apostles could not comprehend until Pentecost. It is where the institution of our Catholic Church fails us. For while clericalism and clerical abuse exists, and our Catholic clergy continue to believe that it is all about "them" on the altar, on the ambo, or administering the sacraments, they fail in the mission of Jesus and gravely harm our true "Church"... God's "Church."

It is being in that highest frequency of the energy state of love; that of the Father, Son, and Holy Spirit existing as ONE, in the Holy Trinity, that is beyond our human understanding. And it is in loving as Jesus teaches us through the Holy Spirit, that we begin to become one with God; one with "Three." And to understand the power, energy field, and energy frequency of the Holy Trinity and of the Holy Spirit is not required to experience and receive "them."

Does this "all-powerful," "all-loving" energy field of the Holy Spirit require being "announced" to be received?

Do we humans/"priests" control the presence of the Holy Spirit or who, how, when, and how often anyone receives its love?

In August of 2020, a young priest in a diocese of New York who had been ordained three years prior was watching a video of his baptism as an infant. It was a baptism in a "Catholic" Church surrounded by baptized "Catholic" witnesses, by a "Catholic" deacon, who was even perhaps nervous. The priest noticed in the video that the presiding Deacon used the words "We baptize you," rather than completing the ritual "We baptize you *in the name of the Father, the Son, and the Holy Spirit*." The young priest overpiously and filled with pride as a recently ordained priest, went to his bishop who "determined" that the priest's baptism was invalid, and since only a baptized Catholic can be ordained, so was his ordination. Since being a priest is not required to baptize, baptisms he had presided at were considered to be okay, but all other sacraments he administered in his three years as a priest had been invalid. So they began attempting to contact everyone who "believed" they had been married by the Church, "believed" they had been absolved of sins in the confessional, and "believed" they had received the Eucharist at mass celebrations had all been invalid and required action. The young priest even asked his mother to return the cloth, which is normally used on the hands of the priest at his ordination and presented to the new priest's mother. The diocese made arrangements for the "priest" to be rebaptized, reconfirmed, and soon after, reordained. However, I don't even want to contemplate imagining the loss of peace, the anxiety and pain that were imposed on many of the faithful Catholics and their families after being informed that all the previous ceremonies and sacraments administered by that "priest" had all been a "sham."

Trinitarian baptism is an important part of our Catholic faith, which distinguishes Christian baptisms from baptisms of other non-Christian religions, but I know deep within my heart that belief in the Holy Trinity is part of our faith, part of what we **know** deep within our hearts, and is not merely "<u>words.</u>" The words of the ritual are important, but if there is a human mistake, is the sacrament, <u>which is from God</u>, invalid? The Church teaches that the priest does not need to be holy for the Eucharist and any sacrament (that is from God, not the priest) to be legitimate and valid. <u>Is a human mistake more fatal than actions of an "unholy" priest?</u> Did the church fail in the preparation of the parents and godparents of the "innocent, love-filled" infant that made the baptism invalid? Would it have made a difference if the one being baptized was an adult and fully understood Christian Trinitarian baptism and the mistake that was done by the minister?

Was the pain that was inflicted by priestly arrogance and "lack of faith," to so many, who had been living <u>faithful</u> loving Catholic lives, justified?

Was the cause of Christ fulfilled by <u>invalidating</u> sacraments, which had been administered <u>and</u> received in love with <u>heartfelt</u> "Catholic" belief and intentions?

As Catholics, the Mystery of the Holy Spirit may be beyond our human understanding, but almost all true Christians understand and have experienced the _**power**_ of the Holy Spirit.

Do people of any religion, who do not comprehend, nor believe in, nor may have ever been exposed to, the incredible "love" of the Holy Spirit, still receive the Holy Spirit?

Again, each of our individual answers to all these questions is between each of us and God and depends on the authenticity of our individual level of faith.

One thing is certain, though, if we believe completely in God and the Holy Trinity **while our Catholic clergy strive to legitimize their priesthood in self-interest and with abusive arrogance, they destroy their credibility as "priests."**

We know also that the Holy Spirit is of major significance in the baptism of Jesus and the beginning of his ministry on earth, in His disciples receiving the flame of discipleship on Pentecost, and in all Christians receiving the Holy Spirit in each of our disciplines and lives with God.

> *"When the time for Pentecost was fulfilled, they were all in one place together. And suddenly there came from the sky a noise <u>like a strong driving wind</u> and it filled the entire house in which they were"* (Acts 2:1–2).

Without any doubt whatsoever, the Holy Spirit is a gift of the love of God, and sometimes, perhaps even a gift received through divine intervention and redemptive grace for **<u>all</u>** people of God including **<u>unholy</u>** priests at the altar in the **Sacrament of God's love, the Eucharist,** which priests do **<u>not</u>** "control."

Although I personally struggle with portions of the Old Testament regarding human sacrifices and of "fearing" the <u>loving</u> God, there is a beautiful correlation in the account of the testing of Abraham with the baptism of Jesus. Abraham was of course, the ancestor of Joseph, the earthly father of Jesus. In the account in Genesis, God says, *"Abraham!"… "Take your son Isaac, your only one, whom you love" [and] "offer him up as a burnt offering"* (Gen. 22:1–2). As a "father," Abraham must have been experiencing unimaginable pain to obey.

Abraham's "beloved son" who had no idea where his father was taking him obediently asked, *"Father! Here I am* [I did as you asked and have everything we need] *where is the sheep for the burnt offering?"* (Gen. 22:7).

After they reached the mountain, Abraham built an altar, and tied up his son. When Abraham took out his knife to slaughter his most loved son, the pain Isaac must have been feeling thinking his father had betrayed him, must have been excruciating as was also the pain of Abraham. God gratefully, through the angel, stopped the sacrifice of Isaac and provided a ram caught in the thicket to be sacrificed instead. Isaac would live to be the father of Jacob. But little did Abraham know that his "beloved" earthly great-great-great-great-GREAT-grandson would one day be Jesus.

Many years later, when Jesus was baptized and came up from the water, the Holy Spirit descended from the heavens, which were opened for Jesus and a voice came from the heavens, *"This is **my** beloved Son, with whom I am well pleased."* This time it was God, sacrificing and surrendering His only Son, the earthly descendant of Abraham. Jesus began his ministry, and would soon be sacrificing Himself for each and every one of us. In His earthly pain, *"My God, my God, why have you forsaken me?"* (Matt. 27:46).

After His crucifixion and resurrection, **the directive of Jesus from "Galilee" was to go out to the world and <u>continue His mission</u>:**

> *"Go and make disciples of all nations, baptizing them in the name of the Father and of the Son and of the Holy Spirit, and **teaching** them to obey everything I have commanded you"* (Matt. 28:19–20).

We **teach** what we learn from Jesus <u>by the example of our lives</u>, whether we wear a collar or not.

When one <u>chooses</u> to wear a collar, though, it comes with making a promise, a promise to service <u>for the cause of God</u> at all costs to himself, <u>devoting his life to God</u> as a "priest" **in humbleness**.

Jesus kept His promise to send His Spirit, to be with ALL of us, to be in ALL of us, to ignite the souls and hearts of ALL of us, and to guide ALL us, whether we <u>choose</u> to follow Him and continue His mission or not; and whether we wear a collar, **or not**.

The role of our clergy is to continue the mission of Jesus, to teach what they've "learned" from their studies of the teachings of Jesus, and to help guide us on our journey and road to heaven. But a "teacher" cannot teach what **he himself** has yet not learned; and a "guide" cannot help us get to where **he** does not yet know the way.

May we always be reminded that <u>nothing</u> that comes from the **Love of God: the Father, Son, and the Holy Spirit**, is <u>controlled</u> by our Catholic bishops, priests, and clergy.

May we pray for our Catholic Church.

Our Pre-Human Life

Many of us believe, or know, that God knows each of us intimately and by name, long before we are even conceived and born into this world. We were each created eons ago from within the love of God, and with <u>His</u> plan for each and every one of us. God, our "Father," knows and loves us perfectly and completely.

The *Oxford Dictionary* defines "passage" as *"the act of moving through, under, over, or past something on the way from one place to another."*

As we each begin our individual passage, we are conceived with an empty slate with nothing more than God's complete and perfect love. At that moment of conception we all are literally created perfectly equal, for, from, and in the folds of God's love.

Through the ages, different religions have held varying beliefs of when the soul enters the human body, whether it is preexisting, at the moment of conception, or during the days following conception as the fetus becomes a viable living being. The Catholic Church does not teach or pretend to know when the actual moment of "ensoulment" occurs, and teaches that the moment a human being is conceived is a miraculous gift from God and should be protected.

It is interesting, though, that "ensoulment" and abortion is an issue that has shown papal fallibility, with popes retracting previous papal positions and doctrine. During our early Church, there was a distinction between an "animated" and "unanimated" fetus. With discrimination, the differentiation was even held by the Church that the soul infused males at forty days and females at ninety days. Abortion has always been considered wrong and sinful, but until the soul entered the body abortion was not considered "murder" subject to various degrees of "punishment" and excommunication. The current disputes within the institution of our Church are whether priests vs. bishops are extended rights to forgive abortion depending on the situation and conditions. Nevertheless, even prior to the sixteenth century when the "animation" of the fetus was reconsidered, and doctrine was modified, it has been maintained that conception is to be protected and considered a "blessed" moment.

But regardless of when that exact moment of "ensoulment" might be in the powerful miracle of creation, when the "new" human "being" becomes a human "person," and we begin to think and feel and love on our own, with our own hearts, minds, and souls, our individual passage begins.

When anyone, including a priest is abusive and hurtful, especially repeatedly, and with little if any sense of feeling and remorse, the expression is often used: "That person has no soul." However, we know completely that God is present always and everywhere, and that we are each created equally lovingly. We are each lovingly created with a soul, a part of God within us; even those of us who may later choose to not be "Christians" and to follow Christ. We are each also lovingly created with the gift of free will to choose whether to live in God's love, or not.

Given everything we believe and know, it would be impossible to live without a soul.

Can we "sell our souls"? It would appear that is what our clergy do as they choose clericalism and pursue exaltation and abuse as priests. But only God can separate us from our souls, which He would never do. With a "loving God" and with our souls lovingly created and bestowed to us, our souls are indestructible and with us always. With human arrogance and fallibility, we can, however, I believe, choose to ignore and betray our souls, and to betray and deeply hurt God in His overabundant love and mercy that is beyond our understanding. If we choose betrayal, the shame we will endure when we meet our loving Father face to face, must be beyond our human imaginings.

When each of our special time to be born as a human being arrives, we come into the world to conditions beyond our control, literally forced on us <u>as a blessing</u>, and <u>nothing less than a miracle</u>. And we come not alone, but with our loving God and "Father" in our souls. As Catholics, it should be within our capability to understand the concept that it would be unimaginable that a loving God would create us without the seed planted within us of His amazing gift of free will for our passage. The gift of free will for us to embrace our soul and choose to become who God made us to be…or not. Only a **loving** God would create man with free will. With a tiny spec of DNA within us to set the direction for the start of our passage and all the earthly external forces and "evil human desires" to come, we're born with the God given gift to choose between right and wrong. However, we come into the world <u>precharged</u> with innocence, goodness, and God's love to set us on our way.

Fr. Ron Rolheiser, of the Missionary Oblates of Mary, describes a "legend" beautifully in his books and reflections:

> *There is an ancient legend that holds that when an infant is created, God kisses its soul and sings to it. As its guardian angel carries the soul to earth to join its body, she also sings to it. The legend says God's kiss and his song, as well as the song of the angel, remain in the soul forever—to be called up, cherished, shared, and to become the basis of all of our songs.* (Fr. Ron Rolheiser)

But is this really only a legend?

The Child Is Born

Animals are born with an innate instinct to survive and live. Scientific studies have found that all mammals, with mammary glands for the mother to nurse their young, including such as whales and dolphins, come with the ability and sense to love and be loved. At conception, God passes the new "creation" to the mother, who literally, physically, and emotionally gives of herself to her fetus and newborn and provides the first example of "earthly" love. Human beings, are born innocent, vulnerable, and helpless with the <u>need</u> to be cared for, to love, and to be loved; but with the full ability to think, reason and make choices including whether or not to follow the teachings of Jesus and strive to live in God's love. What a powerful, heart-filling testament that God **<u>chose</u>** to come to us with so much love, and to be born human, as Jesus, in that same way, two thousand years ago. His greatest command to us was to love one another as He loves us, a tough command to sometimes follow.

As infants we "take in" all our surroundings and the emotions of those around us. As we grow, our lives are formed and defined by: location of birth, our race and ethnicity, the physical and financial health we're born into, the education afforded us, our parents, family, friends, our experiences, triumphs, failures, joys, sufferings…every experience of our lives and who we interact with. Even what we learn or don't learn through our "priests." Without sometimes even being aware, our lives are formed with unintentional biases. We begin to be pulled by the *"desires of the human heart* [which] *are evil"* (Gen. 8:21). With our gift of free will, once we begin to learn to walk and talk and think for ourselves, we get to choose the road straight ahead or to turn right or left, between what is morally right and wrong with the directions we are given, and even to learn from those choices we make…rightly or wrongly.

We are created by God with a purpose; our own individual journeys for His mission. In God's mission for each of us, is intertwined our charge to be who God created us to be, not what our upbringing or society nurtures us to be. When anyone is abused, in any way, that charge may become more difficult or even derailed. It is in that process and challenge of becoming who God made us to be, that we begin to truly get to know ourselves and can experience true "shalom" within. St. Augustine was convinced that coming to know ourselves is how we begin to truly know **God**.

"O God, let me know myself, let me know You" (Prayer of St. Augustine).

As we welcome **God** within us, allow Him to guide us, with all our own human flaws along the way, but now, <u>with Jesus's example</u>, we continue to move God's mission forward by <u>our</u> example of Jesus within <u>us</u>.

When we **believe,** that the desire to be a part of moving God's mission forward comes with the highest form of commitment and sense of "calling," we give and receive the designation of **"priest."**

When what the "priest" preaches **differs** from the life that he lives, and results in abuses of the collar or in harm being inflicted to those he claims to serve, being <u>a "priest" is no longer a commitment</u>

to following the teaching of Jesus. The "ordained" man has <u>chosen</u> merely a "title" rather than a "vocation," and <u>fails</u> as a true "priest" and harms "priesthood" within our Church. That should never be acceptable to "Catholics" within our church family.

Melchizedek

YOU ARE A PRIEST FOREVER?

You are a priest forever according to the order of Melchizedek.
—Hebrews 7:17

Where does this statement and belief, that pumps the egos of priests, and promotes elitism, clericalism, and clerical abuse, come from?

Who is this guy Melchizedek?

There is not much written in biblical accounts regarding Melchizedek, who only appears twice in the Old Testament; in Genesis and in the Book of Psalms. In Genesis,

> *After Abram returned from defeating Kedorlaomer and the kings allied with him, the king of Sodom came out to meet him in the Valley of Shaveh (that is, the King's Valley).*
> *Then Melchizedek king of Salem brought out bread and wine.*

He was priest of God Most High, and he blessed Abram, saying,

"Blessed be Abram by God Most High, Creator of heaven and earth.

And praise be to God Most High, who delivered your enemies into your hand."

Then Abram gave him a tenth of everything.
(Gen. 14:17–20)

There is a lot of controversy and debate on who Melchizedek really was, as well as regarding the account in Genesis of the King of Sodom who comes out to meet Abraham then disappears, and immediately, the king and priest of Salem named Melchizedek greets and blesses Abraham.

When Abraham arrived to the land of Canaan, the general opinion of Jews is that Jerusalem was known as "Salem." Jerusalem was located on the Eastern Hill of the Judean Mountains. The south end of the hill is where Melchizedek is said to have greeted Abraham; the north end (temple mount) is where Abraham is said to have later taken his son Isaac when he was tested by God.

The original name of Jerusalem was *Yerushalem*; it is said that "*yeru*" means "cornerstone" and "*Shalem*" means "peace" and was the God they worshiped in the City of Melchizedek; so Jerusalem was considered the cornerstone of Shalem…,the cornerstone of the world when it was created by God.

The Canaanites controlled Jerusalem for about six hundred years. The fact that Abraham, the Hebrew patriarch, had been blessed by Melchizedek and paid him a tithe was of major significance for the

SHADOWS on Our Catholic "Church"

Canaanites and Jebusites for which they took claim of Melchizedek being superior to Abraham. In Jewish and other traditions, the older and higher ranking in families and communities bless the younger and lower. Jerusalem was later invaded by the men of Judah and the Jebusites took over for about four hundred years during which they built a wall around Jerusalem. In about 1000 BC, David led an invasion evidently entering through the water system, took over the city, and became king. The "City of David" then became the capital of the Jewish Kingdom and the descendants of Abraham continued there. Which was why Joseph, the earthly father of Jesus, was born in Bethlehem/Jerusalem and ironically, so would Jesus.

Melchizedek was considered to foreshadow Jesus the Messiah and eternal priest and king, but since Jesus was not a descendant of Aaron, under the laws of Moses, Jesus would never have qualified for Jewish priesthood. Only Levites could be priests, and non-Levites be kings. While Moses was leading the Israelites, his brother Aaron had the responsibilities of the religious leadership. As leaders of the Jewish religion, the Levites were the most important tribe of Israel. It was believed that the Arc of the Covenant was in the Jerusalem temple, and priests would do the rituals, but only "Levite" priests were allowed to do the sacrificial rituals. "Priesthood" was a very important position for the Jews. There are claims in which texts suggest that Melchizedek was the King of Sodom and that the scribes changed Sodom to Salem to disassociate from the evils of Sodom to the holy religious and priestly center of Jerusalem. Other claims further suggest that the scribes created the biblical figure of Melchizedek, or that, for various reasons, including the lack of biblical ancestry and lineage, that "Melchizedek" was simply an honorary "title" (of priesthood), rather than an actual name. "Melchizedek" is said to have meant "king of righteousness" and peace.

The Book of Psalms was written by various authors, for liturgical purposes. Psalms 110 is believed to have been written by David, who as a king could never be a priest, and begins as "A Psalm of David." The psalms were sung in the Jewish temples of Jerusalem to praise God. Regardless of who Melchizedek was, he had no bloodline, no ancestors, no "successors" or "priestly" history other than a "title." However, rather than for praising God, the psalm has been misinterpreted and misused for praising priests and to give priests a throne of royalty, which Jesus denounced. Additionally, while being tested by the Pharisees, Jesus asked them who their "Messiah" was. The Pharisees answered, "the son of David." Jesus, with reference to the psalm of David, responded, *"If David calls him 'Lord,' how can he be his son?"* (Matt. 22:45). Jesus shut them up and removed any relationship between God and human royalty. Many years later in the New Testament, "Melchizedek" from the song of Psalm 110, "A psalm of David," would be used in the Letter to the Hebrews and written, *"It is testified: You are a priest forever according to the order of Melchizedek."*

The letter to the Hebrews, however, is considered to have only been perhaps a homily or sermon. Although it has been claimed to be associated with Paul, neither the actual author nor its audience has ever been confirmed and is not known. What is known, though, is that at the time, the author was concerned of apostasy from the Christian faith, of the demands of being Christian, and of the lack of men pursuing priesthood. The author, whoever that might have been, was attempting to restore fervor in faith through a message, in the <u>attempt of encouraging men into the "priesthood."</u>

An explanation for the "testament" that "you are a priest forever" was clearly described in the Letter to the Hebrews:

> *It is clear that our Lord arose from Judah and in regard to that tribe Moses said nothing about priests. It is even more obvious if another priest is raised up after the likeness of Melchizedek, who has become so, not by a law expressed in a commandment concerning physical descent but by the power of a life that cannot be destroyed. For it is testified: 'You are a priest forever according to the order of Melchizedek.* (Heb. 7:14–17)

The relevant question is, did EARTHLY royalty and position/ status of "king" mean anything to Jesus or to His mission? The answer is and can only be, <u>absolutely not</u>.

What is profoundly sad regarding the positions and self-empowering "titles" held by "Melchizedek" and members of our Catholic clergy is the fact the Jesus Christ never sought nor required "legitimization." Throughout the ages, the Church has used "Melchizedek," a controversial biblical figure, with his clerical "title" and position of "royalty," to legitimize human priesthood within the human <u>institution</u> of the Catholic Church. However, the **only** means of legitimizing our Catholic "priesthood" would be in continuing the mission of Jesus Christ and striving for holiness in **humbleness, <u>not</u> exaltation** within a <u>false</u> sense of royalty.

Any profession, when entered into **not** for the purpose of its title, prestige, or financial gain, but rather with passion utilizing God given talents for the common good, is a "calling" from God…a "vocation." Any **true** doctor, engineer, scientist, lawyer, author, teacher, father, mother, priest, etc., etc., etc. (in no order of importance) will be a "doctor, engineer, scientist, lawyer, author, teacher, father, mother, priest, etc., etc." "**forever**."

Success has no measure of financial worth or of status of a title. Whatever we are each "called" to humbly do with our lives, and which we do with that level of passion, love, and full dedication, is in one's heart, in one's blood, is part of one's soul to do what God created and blessed us to do. For **any and all "TRUE"** professions, including priesthood, to be a "vocation" and "calling," requires to have been undertaken with a fervent desire for the common good (God), not with self-interest or for selfish gain. It is how we recognize a "calling."

Only "GOOD" makes us do what we do well with LOVE.

The French and Japanese have powerful terms to refer to our "reason for being." In French, it is *"raison d'etre."* In Japanese it is *"ikigai"*; *"iki"* meaning life and *"gai"* meaning worth or value. It is the concept of what we do or how we live that gives meaning and purpose to our lives and defines our "reason for being," our reason to wake up every morning.

"Ikigai" is illustrated through the intersection of four circles of our lives. The circle of our life of *"what we love,"* the circle of our life of *"what we are good at,"* the circle of our lives of *"what the world needs"* ("what we do for God and for the common good"), and the

circle of our lives of *"what we can be paid for."* The intersection of what we love with what we are good at is the ***"passion"*** in our lives. The intersection of what we love with what the world needs and is what is for the common good of all, is the ***"mission"*** in our lives. The intersection of what we are good at with what we can be paid for is our ***"profession"*** in life. The intersection of what we can be paid for or make a living by with what the world needs / what we do for the common good, is our ***"vocation."*** If our profession or the passion in our life is utilized for selfish gain, self-satisfaction, and self-interest rather than for the common good and for God, then there can be no true purpose in our lives; there is no true ***"vocation."*** It is where many of our abusive clergy fail in their lives, and fail our Catholic Church.

Abusive clergy might love what they do, they might even become good at what they do, and they might be "provided for" to enjoy a very comfortable lifestyle. However, if what they receive or what they do is with self-interest, selfishness, and more for a select few and for those who are part of their "clique" rather than for God, the common good of all, <u>and</u> in humbleness, there is no true "priesthood." And there can be no *"ikigai."*

The term "forever" in regard to priesthood and to <u>any</u> profession **can only** refer to our "earthly lives." **How we fulfill God's purpose in our lives on earth, is how we get to "heaven."**

To be a "priest forever" **(on earth)**, one first needs to become a <u>true</u> "priest/disciple," without self-interest, personal glory, or repeatedly inflicting harm to any member of the Church and ultimately to the entire Church itself. A true "priest" also is <u>not</u> something anyone performs "part-time," only when one is on the Altar, or when "proclaiming" the Gospel. To be a true "priest," one is obligated to "live" his discipleship and love for God. Abusiveness in any form or magnitude can never be part of satisfying a "reason for being." Abuse, "desires of the human heart are evil" (Genesis).

Our young priest bragged one morning to the congregation in one of his homilies about being a priest forever and his hopes of continuing to be a priest in heaven; a sad statement from a priest, who obviously might not comprehend the true role of a priest. A priest's focus should be becoming true "priests" on earth, striving for holiness, coming to know God, and helping others to know God, in the hope of helping all attain <u>equal</u> everlasting life in God's presence. The personal aspiration and "desire of the human heart," for a self-interest position and title in heaven is nothing more than arrogance, elitism, and clericalism. How can a true "priest" ever think that his personal exaltation would continue in heaven? A true "priest" would ask himself **with humbleness, "What purpose would human priesthood serve in 'heaven'?"** The answer can only be "<u>NONE.</u>" For "Christians," to come to know God through their lives lived in love, to reach "heaven," and to attain eternal life with God, in God's Kingdom, immersed in God's perfect and complete love, directly with God, **is the entire mission** of our earthly, human lives.

Our Catholic "institution" however, fails our Catholic Church in that "mission."

Cardinal Theodore MaCarrick (and others), has been "defrocked" <u>for serious and grave clerical and physical abuses.</u> To be *"defrocked"* simply means (1) that he was stripped of any prestigious hierarchical positions and "titles" which mean nothing except to himself and other priests, of their own prideful "standing" within the hierarchy of the Institution of the Church and means nothing to the teachings of Jesus or to the cause of God; (2) that he cannot publicly administer the sacraments, for which the Church has always taught anyway that a priest is not required to be moral or "holy," for sacraments are gifts directly from God and not the priest; (3) that he cannot wear the priest "collar," clothing or vestments, which is often, unfortunately, the only way a lay person can ever distinguish that a member of the clergy is a "priest"; and (4) that he is cast to a life of prayer and penance with the hope of remorse and reparation, which is what all priests should be doing regularly anyway.

So how can a "defrocked" man who is no longer allowed to hold an exalted title of "bishop," "archbishop," or "cardinal," who is no longer allowed to perform the duties or functions, which are the whole purpose of being a "priest," who has harmed the Church and its members, who has shamed the institution of priesthood and gravely sinned against the sacrament of holy orders, the teachings of Jesus and the cause of God, all without any show of remorse, still considered a "priest" by the Church Institution? This destroys credibility of "priesthood," and validates that CLERICALISM, **the root cause of evil in the Church,** LIVES ON.

The pre-Vatican II "claim" of an "indelible mark" on the soul of priests is also one of the underlying causes of harmful clericalism. **All** souls are perfect and equal of God's love, and all true Christians, true followers of Christ, whether a priest or not, have the identical "indelible mark" of God's LOVE on their souls and hearts. God would **never** discriminate and preferentially mark any soul. But what unholy or "defrocked" priests or bishops do have, and leave, is an indelible mark (stain) on their successors, on those they have falsely mentored and provided example to, and to our Church. That "indelible mark" on anyone who harms the Church or any/every single member who they harm and cause to withdraw from their Church, is the shadow and stain they cast on our entire Church.

Catholic Priests are only "Priests" (**on earth**) while and **only** if they live their lives (**on earth**) as examples of the teachings of Jesus for the cause of God, and as reflections of God's light. This can **only** occur with authentic humbleness.

Jesus was a "rabbi." **"Rabboni."** In His earthly life, Jesus was not a "priest." By Jewish custom, rabbis were not usually "priests" (who were "Levite" descendants of Aaron). Rabbis (including Jesus), were **lay teachers/ministers**, and men were not considered mature adults to minister until they were thirty years old. The apprenticeship period required to be a minister was about three years, which the apostles "accomplished" as they walked with Jesus for three years before His crucifixion. Numerical significances in the Bible are intriguing and profound. **Did**, however, the apostles and disciples learn from Jesus, or was the Holy Spirit required to enlighten them? **Do** our current day "priests" learn from Jesus, or is the Holy Spirit required to enlighten **them**?

Any insecure "man" with aspirations of being revered and exalted, can become a "priest," but only with <u>humbleness</u> can a priest become a true "man" of God, mature enough to comprehend and respond to the teachings of Jesus.

*May we all pray for "true priesthood" and that God will enlighten and provide wisdom to the institution of our Church for the vision and guidance to reform the Church and members of our Clergy who inflict harm, destroy their credibility as "priests," and to whom being a "priest" is nothing more than a title for its prestige, elitism, clericalism, and clerical "benefits." Reform that is needed: for the common good of our Church, for the mission of Jesus, and for the cause of God. And may we all pray that one day humbleness and the capacity to love by "priests" may <u>**increase**</u> rather than deteriorate, as time progresses in each of their lives as "priests." **Amen.***

What Is a "Catholic"?

So what is a "Catholic"?

What is the meaning of the word *Catholic*?

Jesus and the apostles were Jews. *"You are Peter, and upon this rock I will build my church" (Matt. 16:18).* In the words "my church" was Jesus referring to the "Catholic Church," or to the "Kingdom of God"?

Did Jesus form the **institution** of the "Catholic Church"?

The all-loving, all-inclusive God many of us have come to know, hopefully as "Catholics," but definitely as "Christians," would never exclude any group, religion, or institution that serves the **true** cause of God—whether "Catholic" or not.

After Jesus was crucified, the ministries of Peter and Paul went into Antioch, one of the three major centers of the Roman Empire. The ancient city of Antioch has a heavy history; once part of ancient Syria, it was later annexed by Rome and was eventually taken over by the Huns and Turks. In 1939, it rejoined Turkey with much of its physical history already destroyed. Antioch was approximately three hundred miles north of Jerusalem and roughly two thousand miles, many days travel from Rome. Between the two landmarks was a very important trade route. Under Constantine, Antioch was of major importance to the rise of Christianity. Antioch even functioned as an educational center for biblical studies.

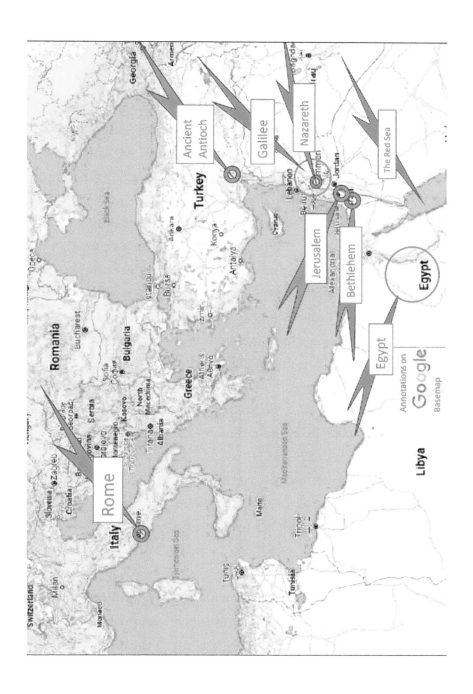

It is interesting that Peter, as is obvious in his betrayals of Jesus and in other accounts, was not a courageous man and was a man subject to bad tempers. The night Jesus was arrested, it was Peter who in fear and anger drew a sword and cut off the ear of Malchus, the slave and servant of the high priest Caiaphas. Had Jesus not stopped the confrontation, picked up the ear and healed Malchus, we can only imagine what might have become of Peter and how the history of the Church might have changed. Divine intervention kept the fulfillment of scripture moving forward. But immediately following this, another miracle in front of his eyes, Peter then cowered at the temple gate and denied knowing Jesus. Peter never aspired to head any community in Jerusalem by himself, much less that of a large universal church. Peter was not a grand personal, spiritual, or ruling presence; he was a simple Jew from Galilee. For Peter, not being a Roman citizen, being uneducated, and not having the command of the Greek language, it must have been difficult for him to be in such an important city of the Roman Empire where Aramaic in the "church" was slowly fading away. So how could Peter have much of a role in this "church"?

After Pentecost, transformed by the Holy Spirit being thrust upon him, his major role became his faith in Jesus Christ, toward the "foundation" in the beginnings of our "church."

It was in Antioch where the name "Christian" was given to the followers of Christ…"Christ people" (Greek translation from "Christos"). The first "Christians" remained in Jewish communities and continued practicing Judaism and its Jewish practices; but one belief "Christians" remained resolute to, was in their faith and belief in Jesus Christ.

Between Peter the apostle to the Jews, and Paul the apostle to the Gentiles, though, there were heavy conflicts about those Jewish laws and the conversion of the "pagans." Eventually after the destruction of the second temple by the Romans, the Jews and Christians severed ties. About thirty years after Jesus was crucified, and about two years apart, both Peter and Paul were martyred in Rome. There are some who believe that Peter was in Rome only at the end of his life, where he asked to be crucified upside down, not feeling worthy to be crucified in the same position Jesus was. It is our faith that tells us that the relics of a male, archeologically determined to be between sixty to seventy years old that are under St. Peter's Basilica in Rome are those of St. Peter.

Paul's ministry was extensive. After Paul was arrested and imprisoned, his trial is said to have lasted two years before he was martyred. On June 29, 2019, Pope Francis presented the Church of Constantinople a reliquary of fragments of "St. Peter's" bones, which, for centuries, had been revered by popes on the altar of their private chapel at the Vatican. The reliquary was presented not as a gift from Francis but as a "gift from God" and a major prophetic gesture of church unity and of the brotherhood of Peter and Paul. Pope Francis obviously recognizes that the Holy Spirit was guiding all the apostles as they dispersed for "Christians," not solely Peter.

With the reputation that the Antioch church had been founded by the apostles of Jesus, the bishops of Antioch were extremely influential regarding church matters. Ignatius, who was the bishop of Antioch and a theologian is credited for beginning the formation of dogma and the hierarchy structure within the Catholic Church and subsequently the beginning of a false sense of power to bishops. Priests, "presbyters," were basically assistants to the bishops and could only administer communion with authorization by the bishops. About forty-five years after the execution of Paul, Ignatius was also arrested and taken to Rome to be executed in the Roman arena. On that long trip to Rome, he wrote letters which became highly regarded by the church. It was within those letters, that the Greek word *katholiko* (Catholic), meaning the "universal, whole church" was known to be used. Ekklesia katholiko would later in Latin be referred to as "ecclesia catholica," the "Catholic Church," the "universal assembly." It is difficult to believe, unfortunate and striking that not until the years 1962 to 1965, some 1,851 years later, that Vatican II (Sacrosanctum Concilium), promulgated under Pope John XXIII / Pope Paul VI, would give the "assembly" a place in Church doctrine. To date, "Vatican II" has yet to be fully implemented, due to clericalism, elitism, pride, and downright arrogance and failure of our Catholic clergy.

Jesus, a Jew, criticized the Jewish temples, the Pharisees and religious leaders of the time. They, however, believed, fervently, that they had always been doing the right thing; including crucifying Him. The biblical accounts of the life and teachings of Jesus, including His criticism of the temples, Pharisees, and high priests, show that God's "Church," His "Kingdom of God," was **not intended** as an "institution" centered on a bishop but rather as a "way of life" of "believers" centered on God.

Ultimately, though, Peter fulfilled Matthew 16:18–19, through his **belief** and **faith** in "Jesus Christ." The "institution" of the "Catholic Church" would be formed later by other humans, through centuries of human problems, errors, scandals, and abuses of many, as well as through the profound faith, personal sacrifices, devotion and love of many others. I believe, though, that theological beliefs based on the teachings of Jesus Christ, the belief and faith in Jesus as the Messiah and Son of the Living God, through the institution of the Catholic Church for the "cause of God" might make Jesus a "Catholic," but not at the exclusion of other religions where common beliefs are shared and not with "Catholics" ignoring the abuses by our Catholic Institution. If Jesus were to become incarnate to the world today, I believe that Jesus would criticize the "Institution" of the Catholic Church and its current day divisive "temples" and "high" priests, for its egregious abusive flaws toward continuing the teachings of Jesus and "mission" of Christ.

If we embrace the teachings of Jesus, it is obvious to us that Jesus never intended his apostles, disciples, and future bishops and priests to continue his mission with any form of clericalism or false sense of royalty. All Jesus asked of us in "God's Church" was to continue His teachings <u>humbly</u> and learn how to "love." Two thousand years of a "church" and man-made doctrines do not alter His mission or how humans respond to it. Would Jesus again be "crucified" via today's methods, by our "high bishops/priests" and those who still do not understand the "mission"?

Many present-day Catholic Christians, "Christ people," especially those who have experienced or witnessed abusive and hurtful actions by the religious members of our Catholic institution, as well as anyone who understands how the Church fails the people of God, pray for reform of the institution of the Catholic Church to become a "Church" that follows the teachings of Jesus and leads to the

Kingdom of God, the "ekklesia katholiko," which many "Christians" deeply love.

As this new "church" evolved between Antioch and Rome, why was primacy given to Peter?

The Primacy of Peter

HOW DID BISHOPS (POPES) TAKE CLAIM TO THEIR SUCCESSION OF PETER?

The Chair of St. Peter (against wall behind the altar), Rome 2019.

During the early years after the crucifixion of Jesus, as Christianity blossomed secretly amidst persecutions, "church" assemblies were held in private homes; large groups would meet in larger homes and private warehouses and other buildings. As more and more gatherings occurred and more and more bishops evolved, so did the mission for unity and for a universal church, where many communities were beginning to do their own thing.

There is nothing really written whether Peter was ever a bishop of Rome. The first official bishop of Rome and second official head of the Church was Linus who interestingly had been ordained by St. Paul. Not until Constantine, emperor of Rome in the fourth century who had become a Christian and favored Christianity, had anyone had such a great impact on the Church. After Constantine legalized Christianity, construction of church buildings began including the Lateran Basilica, and the Basilicas of St. Peter and St. Paul. But with that blossoming of legalized Christianity, huge church buildings, wealth and power in the Church of Rome began to be a major problem, and for the next thousand years, the position of the head that came to be known as "pope" would be plagued by greed, corruption, and abuse. The position of pope would be elected, appointed, bought, sold, and even murdered, for the opportunity of power and abuse that came with it. One account alleges that Pope John XII, who was considered to be one of the worst popes, was murdered by the husband of a woman he was caught having an intimate sexual relationship with. During the growth of the church there have even been two and three popes at the same time with each of their own "followers," vying for the "position" of authority and superiority. And it was precisely for some of the challenges that would rise by political appointments and immoral bishops of Rome in the position and authority of being "pope," that the primacy of Peter through the Petrine Theory had been made the official position of the Church to establish the lineage of the "universal" church and to maintain a form of legitimacy in its organization.

In the accounts of Matthew 16:13–20 just before Jesus began his predictions to the disciples regarding his forthcoming passion and to leaving them, he asked the disciples, *"Who do the people say I am?"*

After disappointment in their answers of many "nonbelievers," Jesus asks them, *"But who do __you__ say I am?"*

When Peter answers, *"You are the Messiah, the Son of the living God,"* and Jesus responds, *"Blessed are you Simon… For flesh and blood has not revealed this to you, but my heavenly Father."*

"You are Peter, and upon this rock I will build my church."

This account of Jesus embracing Peter's **BELIEF** is a basis of the Church establishing the primacy of Peter to which bishops of Rome would succeed.

As many religious scholars contend, *"this rock,"* which was to be the foundation of *"my church,"* as referred to by Jesus, was not a specific "person" but was rather the "faith," the "belief" in Jesus as the *"Messiah, the Son of the living God."* Jesus **Himself** was the foundation of His church, which is the "Kingdom of God."

And it was the "church" of Jesus; the "assembly" of <u>everyone</u> they would gather together in His name, that was a "way of life" following the teachings of Jesus on earth, that was the mission that Jesus commanded all "disciples" to follow and to move forward. It was **not** and never intended, to be an "organization" where human men would aspire for position of power and authority **over** those that they would come to gather in His name, or to claim that any power and authority is "given" to them in "God's name." They were to be "examples" of His teachings.

When Jesus began to explain His mission to the disciples, Peter arrogantly took Jesus aside and began to rebuke Him. *"At this, he*

[Jesus] *turned around and, looking at His disciples, rebuked Peter and said…'You are thinking not as God does, but as human beings do'"* (Mark 8:33).

The institution of the Catholic Church which would be built later by human hands several centuries after the crucifixion would survive thousands of years of corruption and abuses by men *"thinking…as human beings do,"* and bishops becoming positions for a false sense of power and "royalty."

All the same faults Jesus criticized the Pharisees and high priests for.

To be a "Catholic" Christian is powerful and profound. It is **not** only "believing in Jesus," and "believing one is a "follower of Jesus"; it is believing in Jesus as the one and only Messiah and as the Son of God, and perhaps most importantly, **believing in EVERYTHING Jesus LIVED and DIED for**, to the point of living by His example.

So as a "Catholic" Church, with a pope who is a "Catholic" Christian and a "successor" of "one" who truly believes in everything "Jesus" stood for (and continues to stand for), how do we truly become part of the Catholic "assembly" (Church)? Through **"PARRESIA."**

By being true "disciples," willing to speak up, stand with Jesus, follow Jesus, and to **not** simply be "bystanders" who run away in fear (and shame), and **betray** Jesus.

Behind the main altar on the west wall of St. Peter's Basilica (illustrated in the image at the beginning of this chapter), is the altar of the Chair of St. Peter, also known as the "throne" of St. Peter. What is believed to be the relic of St. Peter's chair is encased within an incredible monument by the sculptor Bernini. In its encasement, the chair was embellished as a throne, and holding up St. Peter's "Throne," are four large statues of doctors of the Church, who were third- and fourth-century bishops. Although the magnificent monument of the symbolic chair of Peter is sadly and unfortunately, depicted as a "throne" with the "royalty" of bishops, it is at least **BELOW** the beautiful stain glass image of the Holy Spirit as a symbol of hope of spiritual **enlightenment** to the institution of our Church.

One of those statues holding up St. Peter's "**Throne,**" is that of John Chrysostom, archbishop of Constantinople. Archbishop Chrysostom was known to have denounced ecclesiastical and political abuse of authority.

Almost 1,800 years later, "denouncing" ecclesiastical abuse continues to mean nothing and perhaps also, is simply a "political" statement in past and current history of our Church.

How Can Systemic Clericalism, Elitism, and Clerical Abuses Exist and Continue within the Institution of the Catholic Church, if Our Catholic Clergy Truly Believe in Jesus and in His Teachings?

Judas believed in the power of Jesus Christ, yet he betrayed Jesus.

Peter believed that Jesus was the Messiah; yet he denied Jesus three times, deserted Him, fled, and hid.

Caiaphas, the Jewish high priest, believed in "God" believed he loved God accused Jesus of blasphemy (a crime punishable under Jewish law by death), organized the plot to kill Jesus, and believed he was doing the right thing.

The institution of our Church takes claim to popes being successors of Peter. The bishops and clergy of our Catholic Church, though, are the successors of the all the apostles (Canon 375) and disciples of Jesus Christ. No members of the clergy are "successors" of Jesus Christ. As disciples and Christians, bishops and clergy are called to be "followers" of Jesus Christ.

The apostles and disciples lived with Jesus; they witnessed His actions and "life" with their own eyes, and they heard His Words with their own ears. Regardless of any lack of education and refinement, their lives required a level of faith to follow Jesus, **to try** to understand what Jesus was telling them, **to try** to understand what it meant to "follow" Jesus, **to try** to understand and **to believe** Jesus when He told them that He would rise from the dead in three days and send the Holy Spirit to guide them, and **to believe** Jesus when He said that He would be with them always.

Unlike for the initial apostles and disciples, the "HISTORY" of the life and mission of Jesus Christ, SCRIPTURE and the "Holy BIBLE," is already written. Our Catholic bishops and priests already <u>know</u> the history of the birth, life/ministry, death, and resurrection of Jesus Christ that <u>already</u> occurred, and the history of the Catholic Church as it evolved.

IF, one knows the "HISTORY," **IF** one truly believes and follows the teachings of Jesus, **IF** one truly believes in the real presence of Christ in the Eucharist, **IF** one truly has come to "know" Jesus, <u>DOES</u> it **still** require "faith" to believe Jesus on how our lives are to be lived as disciples?

There are no "<u>IFS</u>" written into the Creed; and every "I believe in" should be "I know":

Creed

I (believe in) [**know of**] *God, the Father almighty, Creator of heaven and earth, and in Jesus Christ, his only Son, our Lord, who was conceived by the Holy Spirit, born of the Virgin Mary, suffered under Pontius Pilate, was crucified, died and was buried;*

He descended into hell; on the third day He rose again from the dead; He ascended into heaven, and is seated at the right hand of God the Father almighty; from there He will come to judge the living and the dead.

I (believe in) [**know of**] *the Holy Spirit, the holy Catholic Church, the communion of saints, the forgiveness of sins, the resurrection of the body, and life everlasting. Amen.*

Is it possible to imagine how, if our clergy **"believed in Jesus," "believed in God the Father,"** and **"believed in the Holy Spirit"** <u>concurrently and devoutly</u>, would impact how they would truly follow the teachings of Jesus?

How can systemic CLERICALISM, ELITISM, and CLERICAL ABUSES by our present-day "apostles and disciples"…our bishops and priests within the current institution of our Catholic Church, **exist and continue**, if they truly "have come to know" Jesus, are sincere in their lives as "priests," and truly follow the teachings of Jesus??

It could <u>NOT</u> exist and continue.

The Legacy of Rome

Just prior to the beginning of the COVID pandemic, I was blessed to be invited to Rome by my brother. A beautiful, historic, and even chaotic large city every Christian and Catholic should visit given an opportunity. Rome is an incredible, complex, ancient city built by power, extravagance, and corruption—off the backs, love, and faith of the people of God.

My brother and I arrived in Rome on a Saturday. On Sunday morning, we were visiting the Castel Sant'Angelo at the east end of Saint Peter's Square. From the lookout on the roof, we could see the crowd gathered in the Square; individuals who had probably endured hours in the sun and the shoving of the crowd trying to get a glimpse of Pope Francis. Normally, Pope Francis has his outdoor audience on Wednesdays, and on Sundays he does the Angeles and greets the crowd from his upstairs window without going outside. As many in the crowd were already leaving, my brother and I decided to walk over to St. Peter's. As we walked up the Via della Conciliazione and reached the Square, Pope Francis came by a few feet in front of us. We knew that was a blessing to us, and a good sign for us and our visit in Rome. The following days, we saw Francis two additional times, but from day one, quickly witnessed how well Francis humbly handles his "celebrity" status at "home" while "humanly" exuding a spiritual presence.

After a few days of visiting some of the magnificent temples of stone, marble and gold, many of the large beautiful churches proved to be more "museums" than spiritual churches. I came to prefer praying in the smaller neighborhood churches which usually show signs of neglect and lack of financial support. They are usually dimly lit, empty, and peacefully quiet. The major cathedrals and basilicas always filled and bustling with crowds made up of tourists of all religions, characters, and personalities from all over the world, many of which are rude and push themselves ahead in lines. Priests from all over the world arrogantly parade in their clerics and full length cassocks expecting special attention, privilege, and reverence, taking a sense of ownership of the Vatican. Many magnificent "churches" are museums of the monuments that were obviously constructed more for the glory and legacy of the popes and their grandeur than for the glory of God. Huge papal statues and ceilings glistening with gold trimmed coat of arms of the pope who commissioned or remodeled the "church" monument often overshadow the religious icons. Even on top of the roofs, such as that of St. Peter, are plastered with papal coat of arms (Pope Pius IX, eighteenth century). Despite the misdirection from all the glory which lures many clergy to aspire to rise in the hierarchal ranks and be assigned to them, with the sense of the power it represents, the monuments serve to teach us the history of our Church institution.

Papal Coat of Arms

Roof of St. Peters Basilica, Rome 2019.

When persecution and arena murders of Christians were no longer tolerated by the people of Rome, the Colosseum became a quarry. Stone, marble, and materials, including the marble seats from which Roman senators and royalty would cheer for the persecutions and death of Christians, were extracted from its structure and used for many of the churches and buildings throughout Rome. Through all the corruption and clericalism that built some of our grandest churches, the world, however, gained some of the most magnificent monuments and works of art by artists and maestros whose God given talents were cultivated, developed, and commissioned by abusive church "royalty."

Within the abusive excesses of the magnificent temples, papal castles and "monuments" incorporated with the basilicas and cathedrals, **anyone who truly believes in Jesus won't find God in the gold; the marble columns, floors, walls, and the statues; or in the priceless tapestries, frescos, and artwork**. But we can all find God and feel His presence and blessings in the labor of love of the workmanship, and in appreciating the God given talents in the hands which created the masterpieces within all the grandeur; even if done for the misdirected glory of the powers to be, in the institution of the Church.

Every early pope "in power" commissioned both: established and well-known, as well as young promising artists, painters, sculptors, and craftsmen to memorialize their legacies. The works involved caused competition, envy and jealousy amongst artists, as can be seen even from the Sistine Chapel. But I imagine that each and every one of the artists, developed and learned more about God, Jesus, the saints, and apostles as they mastered their skills to transform canvas, plaster, and marble and into what they envisioned in their minds and hearts, and realized through their amazing, gifted hands.

Pope Julius II had been made a cardinal when he was twenty-three years old by his uncle, Pope Sixtus IV and while a cardinal was alleged to have fathered at least one illegitimate child. He became pope thirty-two years later, through simony which he ironically, outlawed as a method for future papal positions. He is said to have been a man with a very bad temper and who would even be present at the battlefields. Since the Vatican had its own army, it was Julius that created the Swiss Guard and their uniforms designed by Michelangelo. The accounts have shown many that Julius was more concerned about the Church's grandeur than about being a priest. It was Julius, who created the Vatican museums. Pope Julius had commissioned Michelangelo to carve his grand tomb with his statue (which took many, many years). Rafael was asked to paint the story of the Old Testament on the ceiling of the Sistine Chapel, but he refused. So Michelangelo was ordered to paint it. It is said that upset Michelangelo who argued that he was a sculptor not a painter, and was busy with the pope's tomb, but he began the Sistine Chapel ceiling and finished about four years later. About twenty years later, Pope Paul III commissioned Michelangelo to paint "The Last Judgment" behind the Sistine Chapel altar.

In the early morning Sistine Chapel, we were blessed to avoid the crowds, stroll and "breathe in" the ceiling, walls, and "visual" stories of the Old Testament and "Creation" in Genesis. One's breath is literally taken away, as you study in awe the artist's interpretation of the Bible.

While Michelangelo painted the ceiling of the Sistine Chapel, Raphael who was in his twenties, was summoned to paint the frescoes in Julius's library/study upstairs. Raphael became chief architect for Julius II but died mysteriously in his thirties. This once library, the Room of the Segnatura at the Vatican, is brought to life through the enormous frescoed walls. On one wall is the "Triumph of Religion" (spiritual truth); on the other is the "School of Athens" (rational truth). To study the figures captured in the walls, with the meanings and interpretations in their details is awe-inspiring. The painting masterfully depicts Plato pointing to the sky and Aristotle reaching out to the viewer, each holding his own text of philosophy and surrounded by other philosophers, mathematicians, geologists, astronomers (and children), sources of wisdom, truth, understanding and knowing…including the statues within the work of art. But how Raphael played with all the faces is incredible and sheer mastery. Those who have studied the painting teach us that in addition to the Greek interpretation, there is the Christian interpretation, as can be seen at the bottom left hand corner of the fresco. Starting from the left and going to right: the infant Jesus is depicted with Joseph, the child Jesus with Mary, Jesus as the boy at the temple pointing to menorah with St. Matthew, and then the Risen Jesus (in white) with St. John and St. Paul.

"The School of Athens" by Rafael (The Vatican, Rome)

In the painting, Jesus was incorporated with the educated philosophers, mathematicians, scientists, as well as with the apostles, depending on the perspective of the viewer.

It is profound that Raphael painted himself in the fresco looking at the viewer. An amazing painting of ancient teachers who give insight to never being indifferent, continuing to ask questions, listening even to the answers we don't like, and challenging each other. Jesus (and Socrates) was killed for challenging others. Raphael obviously was challenging the viewer.

The extensive masterpieces are also awe inspiring, almost as if created with the hand of God. The Vatican and church "museums" serve to teach us about both the good and bad of our Church history; to inspire us and humble us. It is a shame and mindboggling that most members of the clergy evidently only see a lavish palatial environment with priceless works of art, with a human quest for personal power and self-satisfaction.

Does, however, the abusive nature of centuries of bishops (popes) striving to build the grandest "temples, tombs, and monuments" to their own "royal" legacy and in their self-pride, serve to continue the mission of Jesus and the cause of God? I believe perhaps it does, but not from their failure toward the mission and teachings of Jesus, but rather because of God's redemptive grace to make good come out of human fallibility, weaknesses, abuses, and corruption. How we allow the magnificent works of art in these "temples" of the Institution of our Church to teach us of God's love, is up to each and every one of us as we keep in mind and never attempt to hide, the historic corruption of our "Church."

It is extremely ironic that Michelangelo's fresco of the "Last judgment" was painted behind the Altar of the Sistine Chapel where the Conclave of Cardinals (bishops) gathers as well as crowds of tourists. The painting shows the incredible imagination that was allowed to Michelangelo. Along with many details of the work of art, on the left side of the painting it depicts people helping and pulling others up, including from out of their graves, into heaven; on the right side it depicts people helping and pulling others down into damnation. In the lower center of the painting, it depicts those contemplating the decision through free will. Our Catholic clergy fit on both sides. Each and every one of us is in the center of the fresco with our free will to contemplate who we decide and choose to follow.

Outside the "wall" in Rome, in the area of the catacombs, is the minor basilica of San Sebastiano Fuori le Mura. Walking into the darkly lit empty church, my attention was immediately drawn to an incredible bust sculpture along the side wall. It is the last incredible work by Bernini, which was once thought to be lost but was rediscovered almost by accident within our current century. Before he died, at the age of eighty-one, Bernini created a masterpiece of his favorite subject, Jesus Christ, to whom he is said to have been devoted. He transformed a chunk of marble into an oversized bust of Jesus titled the "Salvator Mundi" with an incredible face and head slightly raised and *"the unmistakable mastery of movement of the hand, raised to bless humanity"* (as the description reads).

The Salvator Mundi, by Gian Lorenzo Bernini,
San Sebastiano Fuori le Mura, Rome.

Tucked away in one of the neighborhoods in Trastevere is the Church of Santa Cecilia. The first church built on the site was built in the third century and later rebuilt. The church, built on top of the house where Saint Cecilia supposedly lived, are also some claims to have been built backing up to the wall of one of the houses where people would gather illegally before Christianity was legalized. It is also interesting that some of the priests who had been assigned to this church later become popes. The frescoes, mosaics, other artwork, and historic remains are impressive.

The number of churches in Rome is mind boggling, and to discover them tucked away in quiet neighborhoods is literally a treasure hunt. The thought of how many Christians who have found haven for many centuries within these monuments and dropped to their knees in their spiritual thirst is a testament to the power of religion and faith. But it is also a sad testament to the centuries of abuse and to what has occurred and continues behind the scenes within the Institution of our Church.

Our Catholic Church has survived not because of the religious institution and hierarchy, which has promoted the abuse of power of bishops and clergy, but rather because of the beliefs, faith, and even vulnerability of the "ekklesia katholiko," the "universal" and entire assembly of those gathered, including, those members of our clergy who authentically aspire to live holy lives, and to follow, teach, and live what is written and taught in scripture, dogma, doctrine, for the cause of God.

As Catholics we should continue to remember that the positions of popes, bishops, and the hierarchy of the Church were initially intended to unify and give consistency to the many Christian gatherings as they began to become a Universal Church. The belief and claim to the primacy and succession of Peter was for "magisterium" of the church by tradition, for the continuation of the love and teachings of Jesus which had been taught <u>directly</u> to the apostles, and which have sustained us through the centuries. The directive of Jesus was to move the mission of Christ and cause of God forward; it was NEVER to promote the belief that any member of the clergy becomes Jesus or the "next thing" to God as clergy falsely believe and promote. The "indelible mark" that clergy claim is God's kiss we ALL receive when created.

All priests, bishops, archbishops (bishops), cardinals (bishops) and popes (bishops) regardless of their responsibilities of their current position/assignment within the hierarchy, are very simply and nothing more than **men**, sometimes from dysfunctional families, who become "priests" promising to serve God and the people of God. None is more important than the other and, any one alone, by the very definition of "Church," has little importance to the Church. Most importantly, **if any "priest" fails in his belief in Jesus and His teachings, he is of little if any value to the mission of Jesus, as a "priest."**

Only when a man wearing a collar believes in Jesus and can be held to higher standards for how he lives his life for the cause of God and, as an example to others, can he be credible and take claim to being a true "priest."

Our young priest in one of his Sunday homilies told the congregation that the only obligation a priest has is to read the Gospel; if anyone doesn't get it or refuses to follow it, that it was then up to God—a sad statement to his vocation and to what is being taught in our seminaries. The obligation of a "priest" extends far beyond that; one of being an example and **inspiration** to others to follow Jesus in love and humbleness, living the gospel, **not** simply reading it. To encounter and witness anyone who is a humble reflection of the teachings of Jesus is contagious.

Can any of us **imagine** what it would be like to be walking with Jesus and hear Him say: *My time with you on earth will soon be over; tell the world about Me and all that I have taught you; I will always be with you, tell and show them by your example of ME?* Can any of us imagine what our Church would be like if our Catholic clergy really understood that?

Any action done in God's name should be for the cause of God. Only in God's name and with love and humbleness should we gather in our church buildings and in our discipleships to continue building our "*ecclesia catholica.*" Our bishop has <u>sadly</u> "claimed" that his faith has come easy for him. We should ALL at times, **question** our faith. What and in WHO, do we really believe in? Perhaps we should all ask our priests/bishops (and ourselves) the question Jesus asked His apostles, their predecessors, and of all of us, as "Christians," followers of Christ:

"Who do <u>YOU</u> say Jesus is?"

"Who do <u>YOU</u> say God is?"

Not by what they(we) preach, but by how they(we) live their(our) lives as examples to those they(we) serve. If there is conflict between words and actions, we have our God given gift of free will to follow Jesus, with <u>other</u> priests or bishops who may authentically demonstrate what they believe in, how they pray, and how they live. Repeating the words of Francis:

> *Tell me how you pray and I will tell you how you live.*
> *Tell me how you live and I will tell you how you pray.*
> *For in showing me how you pray I will learn to discover the God you live.*
> *And in **<u>showing me how you live I will learn to believe in the God to whom you pray</u>**."*
> *(Pope Francis, February 16, 2016)*

As "disciples," we are ALL called to be <u>AUTHENTIC</u> "examples."

The Sacrament of Eucharist
In Persona Christi

This is My commandment: love one another as I love you. (Luke 15:12)

This is My body, which will be given for you; do this in memory of Me. (Luke 22:19)

God is love. The transubstantiation of the bread into God's body and His real presence occurs in, by, for, because, and only, through God and God's love. *"Wherever two or three are gathered together in my name, there am I in the midst of them"* (Matt. 18:20). The disciples were "commissioned" to "go into the whole world and proclaim the gospel (Mark 16:15). *"Go and make disciples of all nations, baptizing them in the name of the Father, and of the Son, and of the holy Spirit, teaching them to observe all that I have commanded you"* (Matt. 28:19–20).

We are <u>ALL</u> called to be disciples.

Disciples, to evangelize, to teach, to inspire, to encourage, all through example of our lives, to receive God spiritually and physically, and become what we receive.

Discipleship, though, comes with conditions (Luke 9:23–27).

We cannot just claim that we are "disciples."

Under Canon 899, *"The Eucharistic celebration is the action of Christ himself and the Church. In it, Christ the Lord, through the ministry of the priest, offers himself, substantially present under the species of bread and wine, to God the Father and gives himself as spiritual food to the faithful united with his offering."*

For the sacrament and celebration of the Mass, the presiding priest is trained: to proclaim the Gospel so that the assembly can listen to, hear, and receive the "Word" of God, to recite the ritual prayers properly, and to guide the assembly for all (including the priest) to receive the Body of Christ in the Eucharist. Following Vatican II, everyone in the assembly is a "participant," <u>not</u> an "observer" of the "celebration and actions" by the priest.

Canon Law asks that the priest celebrate Mass and <u>receive Eucharist himself regularly, every day</u>, to help him, as he is required, **to strive to become holy**.

But the Church, since the time of Augustine and centuries of abusive lives, teaches that it is not required for priests to be "holy" for the consecration to take place.

We know, though, that "love" comes from within; love needs to be both given and received. The priest is human and may be having a bad day, be in a bad mood, angry, physically ill, distracted, or simply, unholy. I find comfort in knowing that the love within the participating assembly is present, and in knowing completely and with certainty, that the transubstantiation is from God; not from the priest. As theologians reflect, "We become what we consume." We receive God to become part of Him. In order for us to be in His love, we are to live in His love.

105

God only, always, and in everything, works only in, through, and for "love"; and the bishops and priests have no control over God, nor over who receives Him, how, or how many times.

Our Church, since the time of Augustine, teaches, and understandably so, that God Himself is available to us whether or not the presiding priest is in the state of love, holiness, or spiritually "present." However, the Church fails <u>fatally</u> to stress that **the priest is never dismissed from his obligation to strive for holiness**.

At a mass to pray and support seminarians, our young EP diocesan priest preached in his homily that "*the Eucharist does not exist without priests*," which, in my opinion, was arrogance at its greatest by any priest, and a horrible statement to declare in the name of God. For it is the priest that does not exist without the Eucharist and actually exists only <u>because</u> of the Eucharist. An "unholy" priest is only physically and not spiritually present. Whether an "unholy" man who claims to be a priest is actually a true "priest" is questionable. Nevertheless, regardless of the priest, God is <u>always</u> present. If the "<u>institution</u>" of the Catholic Church would fall apart and cease to exist, <u>the Eucharist and God's presence,</u> through <u>our "ekklesia katholico" continues to exist to anyone who believes, and wherever "two or more are gathered in His Name."</u>

The "institution of the Catholic Church" and the "Catholic Church" sometimes function as two separate "entities." When any portion of the "Institution" of our Church, such as our local clergy, fails through being corrupt, abusive, or unholy, the "*ekklesia katholiko*" continues in the love and to the teachings of Jesus.

The power and grace of the sacraments comes directly from God, not from or because of the priest. The priest, as a disciple/

106

follower of Jesus, is called to "Go and make disciples of all nations, baptizing them **in the name of** the Father, and of the Son, and of the holy Spirit, **teaching** them to observe all <u>that I have commanded you</u>" (Matt. 28:19–20).

"In persona Christi" is a Latin "pre Vatican II" term that, with humans involved, fosters clericalism and clerical abuse. Before, during, and after the moment of consecration and transubstantiation of the Eucharist, God is absolutely present; as Christ Himself for all who are participating and "present" in God's love, <u>including</u> the priest.

For a religious consideration from the Vatican, I needed to submit a "donation." After repeatedly attempting to send the donation via the Vatican website and unsuccessfully requesting online assistance, I decided to go to my bank and ask what the best way would be to send money internationally. It was recommended that I send a money order, which is cashable anywhere, in lieu of a personal check or cashier's check. I mailed the funds, and a couple of weeks later I received a letter from a Monsignor at the Vatican stating that they had received the "check" and scolding me for failing to follow instructions in sending the funds electronically via their website. He informed me that "next time," they would send the donation check (money order) back to me! It obviously was not that they were unable to easily deposit the funds; but that it was a matter of principle to them. I could only envision an unhappy, bored, overweight man in his black and red cassock angrily shaking his finger at me rather than a happy man of God with a warm smile simply saying "thank you!" and "God bless you." It caused me to consider whether or not I will ever again send another donation.

Sometimes I think that the collar our clergy wear on their necks constricts the blood flow in their hearts from reaching their heads.

What does, however, reach and arrogantly go to the heads of many of the clergy, though, is the self-elevating misinterpretation of "Persona Christi Capitis," in the person of Christ the Head.

For centuries, our human but beautiful "Catholic" Church has struggled with the concept and intent of this Latin term and the divisions that have resulted over thousands of years. In the many letters by Augustine and the Donatists (including those with Petilianus), one can see the extensive controversies that occurred while Augustine attempted to avoid the schism with the Donatists. The Donatists were a fourth-century Christian group originally led by Donatus and which eventually broke from the Catholic Church. The Donatists believed that if a person received a sacrament or was baptized by an immoral priest, that the baptism or sacrament would not be valid nor legitimate, which would require a second baptism. Augustine argued that the baptism, Eucharist, or any sacrament, was not by the priest personally but rather by God Himself, that "*he* [the priest] *gives not what is his own but what is God's,*" and so it didn't matter whether the priest was holy or not. In concept and intent, that was great! In actuality, though, with "human" men as priests, dangerous! Hence, this is one of the reasons our Church continues to teach, especially following the recent exposure of horrible abuse scandal(s) in the church, that priests are not required to be holy in order for the faithful to validly receive the Eucharist or any sacrament from any priest, at any church, anywhere in the world.

But under Canon Law, Canon 276, Clerics are obligated, ***"bound in a special way to seek holiness in their lives."*** We ought to never say it is okay if they are repeatedly not holy or do not strive to be holy. But at least it clarifies the Church's belief that the transubstantiation is by God and not the priest, even though many priests themselves enjoy believing and for others to believe, that they actually become Christ (God). Our Catholic clergy place too much relevance in their own self-importance rather than into <u>God's</u> gift of His powerful miracle of the transubstantiation and to what is happening on the altar at that precious solemn moment in all our blessed lives, <u>including that of the priest</u>. The priest's <u>ministerial</u> role is important only in love and complete humbleness, <u>never</u> in self-glorification and arrogance.

One afternoon at lunch with a group of priests, discussion came up regarding a recent appearance and performance in the city by David Copperfield. One of the older priests said, "*The only magic I know about is the one I have power to do.*" I could only think what a shame that is, how he has lived and continues to live his daily life as a priest as he approaches retirement.

During the life changing Second Ecumenical Council (Vatican II) of 1962 to 1965 under Pope John XXIII / Pope Paul VI, a decree on the ministry and life of priests, "Presbyterorum Ordinis," was promulgated by the pope. Within that decree, the new roles of the priests with the laity was explained. Although they were not totally removed off of their pedestals, they were lowered on them. For the sacrifice of Mass, priests were described as "*acting in the person of Christ <u>as ministers</u>*" and "<u>*asked to take example from that with which they deal.*</u>" In the Eucharistic sacrifice, the priests "*join in the act of Christ.*" Obviously the decree was careful not to imply the priest becomes Christ but rather "<u>*acting in the person of Christ as ministers.*</u>"

But as human beings, the fine line causes opportunity for clericalism and abuse. The perspective of the clergy becomes the self-importance of priesthood rather than the importance of Christ. Their roles and Eucharist are rooted in the scriptures:

> *This is My body, which will be given for you; do this in memory of Me.* (Luke 22:19)

> *This is My commandment: love one another as I love you.* (Luke 15:12)

> *Wherever two or three are gathered together in my name, there am I in the midst of them.* (Matt. 18:20)

> <u>**Go therefore,**</u> *and make disciples of all nations, baptizing them* **in the name of the Father, of the Son, and of the holy Spirit,** <u>*teaching them to observe all that I have commanded*</u> *you. And* **<u>behold</u>, <u>I am with you always</u>,** *until the end of time.*

On April 14, 2010, at the general audience in St. Peter's Square, Benedict XVI <u>attempted</u> to explain persona Christi in saying that since God is always present everywhere, that the priest cannot "represent" Christ and be delegated to speak or act in His stead, so he, therefore, has to act in "Christ's person." In my opinion, one of the most beautiful mysteries of our faith filled lives is continually, humanly misinterpreted and distorted in our neighborhood churches. At that powerful moment of consecration and transubstantiation, God is already present and would instantaneously become present directly in the Eucharist. In Benedict's explanation, God's overall "presence" would disappear once God would become present in the priest or the host. The priest (especially an unholy priest), never "becomes Christ," nor becomes Christ and then vanish into the host as the Body of Christ. There is no transformation of the priest "minister" into Christ.

To believe that God would need to transform Himself into the priest and subsequently into the Eucharist would be arrogant narcissism, the opposite of humbleness. God does not force Himself into anyone, not even into a priest whether holy or not. However, if anything, God might temporarily take the place of the unholy priest as the minister, through divine intervention, which must have obviously occurred on many occasions with unholy priests. If we truly know and love God, and believe in the true *ekklesia katholiko*, we know that it is in the love of the entire assembly, including the priest, all gathered in His Name and in His Love that God makes Himself physically and divinely available to us in the Holy Eucharist.

The role of the priest is not demeaned, the role of the priest becomes that much more important; as a powerful example that **God's love and grace, when truly received, can ONLY inspire humbleness.** That is what I believe is the powerful intent of the Second Vatican Council expanding on the lives of Constantine, Augustine, and other "TRUE" Christians through lives well lived, for God, guided by God, and authentically in God's love.

The priest should be **humbled!** And **inspired!** <u>To desire</u> with all his life, <u>to strive</u> to be holy, not because he is obligated to by Canon Law. AND he should <u>desire</u> with all his life, <u>to strive</u> to **inspire** holiness <u>in others</u>, not through what he says or "reads" or falsely believes comes from simply wearing a collar, but **by the example of how he lives and loves in Christ**…together with the desire to get closer and closer to God, and <u>to come to know God</u> HUMBLY.

Augustine's goal to unite the Church can **only** evolve by priests being humbled rather than exalted. To be humble enough to know that they do NOT receive any magic power, but rather along with the assembly together have a powerful encounter of the heart with God and of His promise "Behold, I am with you till the end of time," as He makes Himself known to **all** of us in the breaking of the bread.

The COVID pandemic of 2020 showed attentive Catholics many things:

One of many is that our clergy demonstrated that they are "nonessential" in regards to our faith and love of God. Our local diocesan clergy were for the most part unavailable and not to be found, especially during the worst portions of the pandemic. Catholics were **denied** the sacraments; **denied** to have funerals, baptisms, confessions, matrimonies, etc., even privately. Complete failure in what disciples/priests are specifically called to do. A couple of the young newly ordained priests were assigned to be the ones to assume the risk when anyone insisted on having a dying loved one anointed.

For the most part, only large donors and "special" members of parishes may have been contacted by priests to simply check how they or their families were doing, or to pray with them. For a majority of the hundreds, perhaps thousands of families grieving the deaths of loved ones, not even one single priest was available for a private, safely administered, service; but six or more priests could always be made available to concelebrate if a prominent parishioner, large donor, or other priest unfortunately died.

Throughout the pandemic, our local Church failed the community horribly.

When Pope Francis's security team was trying to protect him during his initial days as pope from leaving the walls of the Vatican or going into the crowds, Francis was quoted something to the effect of *"if God put me here and wants me here, He'll have to take care of me."* That example and level of faith from our local bishop and priests is nonexistent. Sacraments were shamefully "not available" as safely as possible, through any means.

During the Spanish Flu epidemic of 1918, priests were sent out by Pope Benedict XV to assist the medical caregivers to the sick and dying. During the 2020 COVID pandemic, EP local priests were not even available as <u>spiritual</u> caregivers. The bishop <u>continues</u> to celebrate mass on social media and television for public media attention. Sunday mass at the cathedral is regularly and arrogantly promoted on television commercials as *"The bishop will have a SPECIAL Mass."* As Catholics we all know, EVERY Mass and celebration of the Eucharist is of the same "SPECIAL" category, whether or not the bishop presides as the "priest." What a loss of an opportunity for the entire diocese to get introduced to and celebrate Sunday Mass with all the priests of the diocese rotated at the cathedral rather than the bishop reaching for public face time, calling attention to himself on television, flaunting expensive new vestments and mitres, while pleading for donations via phone or internet. Sadly, even after fully opening churches, Sunday Mass is introduced as a "*production,*" **prerecorded** on Fridays, in an **empty** church.

To <u>not</u> be "allowed" to receive the Eucharist sacramentally implies that the sacrament of faith through both the liturgy of the Word of God, as well as through the liturgy of the sacrament of Eucharist, in the celebration of holy Mass is in essence being <u>demeaned</u> to a theatrical performance and is <u>denying</u> the **presence** and **power** of the **love of God**. As a "theatrical production" in the El Paso diocese, the bishop rolls "production" credits and the list of the "performers" after the completion of the mass. As the television station introduces the "mass," it is physically referred to as a "production" and the commercial sponsors of the "mass" are announced to receive credit and attain their publicity. The "production" then begins and the cameras roll with bright lights focusing on the coat of arms inside the "<u>throne</u>" of our "acting" bishop. The sacrament of mass and the Holy Eucharist **should never** and **can never** in any way be presented as a "production." We thank God for the gift of the "sacrament" that is fully/only received from **<u>God</u>** despite the theatrics and poorly administered celebration by our clergy.

IF **one's presence,** desire, and necessity to participate at Mass via internet or television **is** legitimate, **how** can the Mass, God's love, and the ability to receive God, **not** be legitimate and valid, including sacramentally? With one's faith, God's grace is available to us by simply "reaching to touch the cloak of Jesus," and by our authentic desire for the Eucharist. Too much self-importance is placed by our clergy, into **<u>controlling</u>** what **<u>God</u>** gives freely, abundantly, and unrestricted, with His heart wide open.

The Church's teaching that the Eucharist is legitimately and validly received because it is a gift of God not the priest, regardless of the priest's state of grace is understandable; but to receive the true presence of the God in the Eucharist, <u>also</u> requires the priest and anyone in the assembly who receives the "Body of Christ" to being "truly present." Love must always be both given and received with open hearts…something worthy enough to be repeated again and again.

Perhaps without even realizing, we all have more than likely, sadly, witnessed a priest preoccupied and not fully present during Mass and while administering the Eucharist. Some priests even seem to actually believe that they are the Eucharist "police." Their eyes follow laity all the way back to their pews and have even sometimes chased them, concerned that the Eucharist had not been consumed. By that action, the priest interrupts and compromises the peace of those receiving the Body of Christ as well as his own, and distracts attention away from the Sacrament. If there is a <u>legitimate</u> concern on the part of the priest, perhaps it implies failure on the part of our clergy to the religious/spiritual education within the diocese.

The Body of Christ must in all circumstances be handled with veneration, care, and respect; yet on occasion during mass with the bishop several years prior to the pandemic, the bishop literally tossed the Eucharist into the open hands of those receiving communion to avoid any touch. But the perception the Catholic Church has always given is that God needs **<u>us</u>** to protect **<u>Him</u>** and that only "consecrated" hands (whether holy or not) are worthy to touch God. So the Church locks the consecrated hosts in solid metal boxes (tabernacles). Every time I enter a Blessed Sacrament Chapel to pray, I can almost physically see God sitting on top of the tabernacle with a loving smile on His face, His heart glowing, and His arms extended. Shame on us, to believe that **we** can lock God inside of a box.

Whenever a consecrated host has been stolen for whatever purpose somewhere in the country, including for use in "Black Masses," the term given to satanic worship/desecration, the Church has historically gone ballistic to retrieve the host, even to the extreme point of ransom, rather than simply acknowledging the grave wrong that was done, acknowledging agreement in the "presence" and power that the perpetrator obviously believes is in that host, and that the Church is praying for the remorse and conversion of the culprit(s). Even if only one person participating in the wrong being committed, were to personally experience a sense of the wrong involved and a transformation, the host would have been for the cause of God. Jesus never ran from the challenge or from the evil. Jesus always confronted Satan head on. Jesus was spit on, cussed at, thorned, scorned, mutilated, and crucified. Some theologians have written in reflections that Jesus was more than likely even sexually abused by the Roman soldiers as they were known to have done, to many.

God, does not need us to protect Him; God simply asks us to follow Him, to love one another as He loves us, and to strive to be an example of His presence in us.

Even a few months before the pandemic interrupted our lives as we once knew it, the harm inflicted on me by our El Paso diocesan clergy was so deep that I have been compelled to withdraw from participation at church or attendance at Mass celebrations or association with them; they have completely destroyed their credibility as priests to me within the diocese as a whole. I cannot even imagine what victims of major physical abuse by clergy all over the world have endured, but the indescribable harm to me as a "Catholic" has been tough for me. Not solely from the major disappointment and disillusion in the institution of our church and it's clergy, but an anger from being forced to withdraw from the physical church where I have practiced my religion of choice with family and friends, my entire life. Nevertheless, via internet, I would attend Mass being celebrated at the Vatican with Francis or at churches in other cities and states with diocesan and religious order priests, especially those I have come to know and cherish over the years, as authentic men of God. They do, in fact, exist—<u>most often</u> away from the diocesan order within other more humble religious orders.

One of the powerful aspects about Catholic Mass is that Mass is celebrated in the exact way with the exact same words and rituals, in different languages and with minor cultural adjustments, all over the world. At any given Mass we attend, actively participate, and are truly present, we are celebrating mass with hundreds, thousands, and even millions of other Catholics at Mass(s) being celebrated, even at the exact time, somewhere throughout the world. When we receive the Eucharist, it is at the same table with God and the multitude all over the world as well as with the saints, including our loved ones who have lived and died before us. It is a powerful and awesome part of God's gift to us and of our faith. Via the internet, one can visually and if sincerely and actively participating, can very physically, join others within our Church family at some church anywhere in the world. A profound feeling, connection, and personal encounter **occurs**, if one is truly "present."

I have no idea what the Vatican's current position is (especially since COVID) regarding receiving God sacramentally by anyone who sincerely participates in the celebration of mass via internet or television. Mass celebrations with Pope Francis at the Vatican during the height of the pandemic, were always simple and dignified. No messages were plastered on the screen during communion as they were in the US for the viewer to acknowledge that one could not sacramentally receive God. No restrictions or limitations are placed or implied that it is not a legitimate and valid Mass celebration, and no "production" credits are rolled at the end of the celebration as done by the EP diocesan bishop calling attention to the "performers."

But one thing is certain, we, all people of faith, wholeheartedly believe and know, completely, without any measure of doubt, that <u>no one has a human right to deny God's presence to anyone</u>, that <u>God cannot be kept out by locked doors and closed hearts; or be filtered by cyberspace and the internet</u>. With no restrictions, God and His graces are available to us infinitely and in any way our hearts are willing to receive Him. God will even open the door if we are hesitant or unable to come to Him.

The Institution of the Church needs to keep in mind a few facts:

- The Second Ecumenical Council (Vatican II) under Pope John XXIII / Pope Paul VI, occurred in 1962–1965.
- Internet and the ability of networks to communicate with each other did not exist prior to January of 1983.
- Web browsers did not exist until April of 1993.
- Facebook did not become widely available until September of 2006.

- Although its possibilities have only been realized by humans in recent years of the twenty-first century, God created energy waves, frequencies, quantum entanglement, and cyberspace during the CREATION of the universe; <u>GOD is the MASTER at it.</u> The Institution of our Catholic Church has no control over those forces, how God makes Himself available to each and every one of us, or how, when, and how often we receive Him.

<u>If our bishops and members of the clergy deny, or believe that they can prevent, control, or filter, God's movement via cyberspace or any other means, then perhaps those within the Institution of our Catholic Church believe in a different God than those of us in our "Christian" *ekklesia katholiko.*</u>

I believe in God's presence within the entirety of His CREATION, and I believe completely in the Eucharist and of God's real presence in the Eucharist. Over the many months that I "could not" attend physical Mass, both for the harm inflicted by our diocesan clergy as well as the pandemic, there was a very deep and personal desire and calling to me, for the Eucharist.

One Sunday, prior to the broadcast of the celebration of Mass at a cherished religious order, "true" Catholic Church in Albuquerque, NM, I placed an unconsecrated host I acquired through a religious/church supply, and a small blessed crucifix, on a crystal dish. I actively participated at Mass with cherished friends on my screen. During the liturgy of the Eucharist and the Consecration, I placed the dish on top of my computer in front of the screen. As the priest began distributing the Eucharist, the words "Body of Christ" were clearly audible. With the standard *"amen,"* I consumed the host.

The previous day at dinner, I had burned my mouth and had a bruise on my tongue, which was very physically sore and painful. Immediately upon consuming the host, the bruise and soreness in my mouth from the burn was gone. It had vanished.

In my heart, I "sacramentally," spiritually, and physically received God through the Word and the Eucharist and God's grace. I experienced God's love and a personal encounter with Him.

After the final blessing, I purified the dish rinsing it with water into the soil of a green plant. There was a religious, spiritual peace within me which I had not experienced in a long time. I thank God for Mass celebration and the Eucharist being available with a priest who I know for a fact, strives to be holy, authentic, and humble, and with my "*ecclesia catholico*" "assembly family."

"When religion divides us, our spirituality unites us" (Author unknown).

Within the Major Basilica of Santa Maria Maggiore in Rome, whose construction started in 435 AD and took over one thousand years to complete, the beautiful tabernacle is in the image of a "CHURCH" suspended by four angels. Throughout the ages, though, the entire <u>concept</u> of "God in the Church," of "God in our neighborhood churches," and of how "WE ALL" are the "Church," has been clouded by the "shadows" of clericalism.

As disillusioning as it is to experience the religious shortfalls and failures of our local bishop and clergy with the division and harm it inflicts, I continue to find hope in our Church through Pope Francis, toward the **SPIRITUALITY** that unites our Catholic faith. I believe that Pope Francis has slowly, but successfully been chipping away at the "self-referential Church" he understands exists and described at the beginning of his papacy. If it were not for the self-interest and level of opposition from right wing clergy, supported by overpious laity, advances in the church spirituality and reform within the Church, would be further along.

So what was some of the vision Archbishop Bergoglio shared and described as he became "Pope" Francis?

Spirituality That Unites Christians as Reflections of God's Light

BERGOGLIO'S MESSAGE TO THE CONCLAVE

In the days leading to the conclave of 2013, Archbishop Bergoglio gained the attention of the cardinals in his vision of the state of our Church and its future. Later, the cardinal from Cuba is said to have asked the new pope for any text of his comments to the Conclave. Evidently, Pope Francis agreed to write down remarks as he recalled them; and when asked, also gave permission to release them, which a photocopy was published in the Havana diocesan magazine. Pope Francis also included similar remarks in the inspirational apostolic exhortation, *Evangelii Gaudium* on evangelization.

From those shared handwritten remarks I cite here only portions of the message by Francis's comments that are obviously his belief from his years of prayer and study of scripture, theologians, philosophers, and patrologists, in humbleness. Francis passionately referred to evangelization and the apostolic fervor required for the *"parresia,"* the need of the Church to be bold to *"come out from itself."* If it does not come out of itself, *"it* [the Church] *becomes self-referential and gets sick."* He compared it to *"theological narcissism."*

Bergoglio, Pope Francis, referred to Revelations 3:20 were Jesus is standing at the door knocking and calling to enter, but rather how *"at times* [he thinks] *that Jesus may be knocking from the inside, that we may let Him out,"* and how *"the self-referential Church presumes to keep Jesus Christ within itself and <u>not</u> let him out."* A profound observation by a man who said that the *"next pope"* would need to be *"a man,* **who through contemplation of Jesus Christ and the adoration of Jesus Christ, may help the Church <u>to go out from itself.</u>"** When the Church "is self-referential," he said, *"without realizing, it thinks that it has its own light; it stops being the **'mysterium lunae'** and <u>gives rise to that evil which is so grave, that of spiritual worldliness</u>* (that, according to theologean De Lubac, is **the worst evil into which the Church can fall**): *"<u>that of living to give glory to one another.</u>"* (That spiritual worldliness [which] would attack the Church at its very origin.)

I believe, that <u>only</u> those who truly believe in Jesus and in His teachings, and who love our "true" "Church," can understand or try to understand Bergoglio's profound, profound, acknowledgment. What a shame that all bishops and priests throughout the world, many through arrogance and self-interest, have <u>NOT</u> helped Francis *"help the Church go out from itself."*

May our local diocesan church and many others throughout our world Church, one day see and follow the "true light" to free itself from spiritual worldliness.

Mysterium Lunae

Two years later, in 2015, after being elected as pope and while traveling to South America, Francis would further expand on *"mysterium lunae"* saying, *"As Christians, we compare Jesus Christ to the sun, and the moon to the Church, the community; no one else but Jesus shines of His own light."* He later expanded his remarks further, *"The moon does not have its own light, indeed if it hides from the sun it will be enveloped by darkness. The sun is Jesus Christ and if the Church moves away or hides from him, she will be in darkness and no longer able to offer witness."*

In July of 1991, I was blessed to travel with close friends to the southern coast of Mexico to experience the total eclipse. This phenomenal event of 1991 was reported as *"the most central eclipse in eight hundred years...and...of a magnitude greater than any eclipse since the sixth century."*

Eclipse of July 11, 1991, photos cherished gift from Dave Etzold.

Just before the peak of the eclipse and exposing the incredible "corona" thousands of birds took flight into the sky as if to announce the event from the heaven above. While looking out from coast toward the horizon of the ocean waters, we experienced what appeared as a mesmerizing full 360-degree sunrise during high tide. The umbra, the conical darkest shadow of the moon, travels along a path on the face of the earth approximately a mere one hundred miles or so wide. If one could peek around the moon's shadow, one could have seen the sun. But the rays of sunlight gently pushed the moon aside, and the sun reclaimed command of the sky. A few hours later as evening embraced us, **the moon bowed to the sun and took its proper place in time while it beautifully reflected the sun, and smiled at God's world**. Those of us blessed to experience the humbling phenomenon, with spiritual significance, would never be the same.

On the Solemnity of the Epiphany in 2019 (Vatican document is dated "2018") Pope Francis in his homily said,

> *God's light does not shine on those who shine with their own light. God "proposes" himself; he does not "impose" himself. He illuminates; he does not blind. It is always very tempting to confuse God's light with the lights of the world. How many times have we pursued the seductive lights of power and celebrity, convinced that we are rendering good service to the Gospel! But by doing so, we have turned the spotlight on the wrong place, because God was not there. His kind light shines forth in humble love. How many times too, have we, as a Church, attempted to shine with our own light! Yet we are not the sun of humanity. We are the moon that, despite its shadows, reflects the true light, which is the Lord. The Church is the **mysterium lunae** and the Lord is the light of the world (cf. Jn 9:5). Him, not us.*

The preceding homily is a powerful one, not only from its words, but from continuing to show Francis's belief in Jesus and belief in the meaning of the "Catholic Church," the part of the "Church that is of Jesus." He has continued to stand for the purpose and with the vision for which he surrendered, to become the pope of our Church.

It is difficult to understand and fathom how bishops and priests within our diocese and every diocese in the United States are incapable of embracing this and to being an active part in moving the mission of Christ forward. The above thoughts and quotes of Pope Francis, though, beautifully explain all the corruption, abuses, and harm caused by the clericalism and elitism of our Catholic bishops and priests who truly believe that they have and shine their own light.

Our diocesan bishop and priests publicly claim obedience, and pretend to support Pope Francis, yet by contrary actions, they inflict harm that is more serious than they recognize. They lead our diocese shining their own "light," one that blinds rather than reflects the true, gentle, loving "light" of God.

Pope Francis understands the cause of abuses within our Church. Perhaps he understands it occurs daily in our local diocesan church(s) by our local bishop(s) and priests? May we pray that he will inspire their illumination for *"the possible changes and reforms to be realized"* for the cause of God. Being driven away by our clergy from the Church we love, is painful. It is wrong.

There is a disease in the Church. We know the cause. We know the cure.

Clericalism and elitism fosters abuses of all forms and magnitude. We should be enlightened, inspired, and committed to eradicating the disease and the pain and harm it inflicts. It cries out for our clergy to live the lives for which they claim to have taken vows of priesthood; it cries out for reform of our Church; it cries out for "PARRESIA."

In their blindness, our clergy are chasing the "assembly" out of our "ekklesia." May we all continue to pray with hope, for the Institution of our Catholic Church within our "ekklesia katoliko"— our Catholic, Universal, "Church." THE ASSEMBLY.

The Dualism of Our Catholic Church

Over two thousand years ago, Jesus sent out the (doubting) apostles, *"Go ye out to **all nations,**" baptizing them in the name of the Father, and of the Son, and of the holy Spirit, **teaching them to observe all that I commanded you**. And behold **I am with you always**, until the end of the age" (Matt. 28:19–20).*

When asked and tested by the Pharisees on the "greatest commandment," Jesus answered, *"You shall love the Lord, your God, with all your heart, with all your soul, and with all your mind. This is the greatest and first commandment. The second is like it, You shall love your neighbor as yourself. The whole law and the prophets depend on these two commandments" (Matt. 22:37–40).* After Jesus left the Pharisees, He spoke to the crowds and to His disciples and denounced all the hypocrisies and lives of the scribes and Pharisees.

It is interesting that by tradition of our Church, the Gospel of Matthew is believed to have been written by the apostle Matthew, in Aramaic. Many biblical scholars believe the Gospel of Matthew was written by another author after the destruction of Jerusalem, perhaps in Antioch, in Greek, and much of it based on the writings of Mark. When Herod took reign of Judea, his plan was to kill Peter after Pentecost and had him arrested. The accounts of Luke describe how Peter was saved from prison by angels. Peter then went to Antioch, and ran into Mark. Mark followed Peter and wrote down his sermons. Regardless who is the actual author of the Gospel of Matthew, "Matthew" believed it was important enough to include quite a descriptive account of the dissatisfaction of Jesus. <u>Jesus was known to have been concerned that the Pharisees were an extremely negative example to His disciples.</u>

The accounts of Matthew describe Jesus angrily warning the crowds about the Pharisees and teachers of the law. Jesus warned the crowd to be careful to do everything they <u>tell</u> them (us), but to **not** do what they <u>do</u>, for <u>they do not practice what they preach</u>, that <u>everything they do is done for people to see</u>, that <u>they love the place of honor at banquets and the most important seats</u> in the synagogues, that <u>they love to be greeted with respect</u> in the marketplaces and to be called "rabbi," but that (we) have one Teacher and (we) are all brothers. To not call anyone on earth "father," for (we) have one Father in heaven, and that (we) are not to be called instructors, for (we) have one instructor, the Messiah. That those who exalt themselves will be humbled, and those who humble themselves will be exalted.

Jesus called the Pharisees and teachers of the law "hypocrites!" and "blind fools!" That they shut the door of the kingdom of heaven in people's faces. That they travel over land and sea to win one convert, and when successful they make him twice the "child of hell" as they are.

Jesus asked the Pharisees and "teachers" of the law whether it was the **gold**, or the **temple** that makes the gold sacred, that was more important, and whether it was the **gift**, or the **altar** that makes the gift sacred, that was greater. Jesus told the Pharisees and teachers of the law that they clean the outside, <u>but inside they are full of</u>

greed and self-indulgence, and that on the outside they appear to people as righteous, but on the inside they are full of hypocrisy and wickedness.

Jesus was angry! He called them "Snakes!" "Brood of vipers!" and asked them how they would escape condemnation to hell. The Institution of our Catholic Church did not exist until many years after His crucifixion, but the account in Matthew 23 is powerful. What a shame that our clergy actually believe Jesus directed his denouncement only to **past** "Pharisees."

After the crucifixion and resurrection of Jesus, and enlightenment by the Holy Spirit, the apostles went out to all nations. Slowly, the institution of the "new church" began to develop, and bishops began to literally replace self-righteous Pharisees. In the effort to maintain the growing number of dispersed church gatherings united as a "universal" church, the hierarchy was organized with canons, doctrines, and rules as an "Institution" of the Church. It was intended to keep those of all nations who were gathering "in the name of God" from getting out of control and doing their own thing. However, with the hierarchy and human desire for power, evolved clericalism, elitism, and an "evil" within the new "institution" of the Church.

"Dualism" is defined in *Merriam-Webster's Dictionary* as "a doctrine that the universe is under the dominion of two opposing principles one of which is good and the other is evil."

Our united, universal "Catholic Church" is often two entities our "ecclesia catolico," which are our church assemblies; and the "Institution" of our Church which is made up of the hierarchy. The **"dominion"** of our Catholic Church is often under **two opposing principles**, that of the "teachings of Jesus Christ," and that of "hierarchy clericalism, elitism, and clerical abuses of our clergy." One is practiced under a **principle of good**; the other is often practiced under the **principle of evil** (whether intentional or not).

Which principle do we as Catholic "people of God" choose to follow?

To continue as true "Catholics" in a "Church of Jesus" <u>will our bishops and clergy one day cease in disuniting and driving us away from what was intended as the "universal 'Christian' church"</u>? Why did Jesus choose weak, uneducated, and unrefined men to follow Him? Obviously, for many reasons, but one thing is certain: Jesus never intended anyone to pretend to be spiritual and theological experts to control others; or to pretend and claim to teach about Jesus through "clericalism." The Pharisees already lived that example, and <u>Jesus publicly denounced them</u>. Jesus only asked one simple (but not always easy) task of us to LOVE, to love God completely and to love each other as ourselves.

Clearly we can hear Jesus as He <u>gently and lovingly</u> asks each and every one of us:

> *Do you not yet understand or comprehend?*
> *Are your hearts hardened?*
> *Do you have eyes and not see; ears and not hear?*
> *And do you not remember?"* (*Mark 8:17–18*)

<u>**When**</u> do we stop being **indifferent "bystanders"** to the abuses of our Catholic clergy and remember why Jesus asks us to follow

Him? **Or** <u>do we continue to turn the other way</u>, <u>abandon Jesus</u>, <u>blindly follow our priests, and support their clericalism</u>, <u>and continue to harm our Church?</u>

Human abuses began with the creation of man. Clericalism and clerical abuses began and have continued since the Institution of our Church was formed. When does clericalism and abuses of the gift of priesthood **<u>stop</u>** so that the true Church can **<u>begin</u>**?

Perhaps we might be better off reverting to "pre-Constantine" assemblies in our homes and to <u>welcome</u> and <u>loving</u> gathering places away from our church "temples," to actively practice as Catholic "<u>Christians</u>" with and in God's love?

Where Do We Go from Here?

When our clergy abuse the **GIFT** of priesthood in any form/magnitude, give themselves such self-importance through clericalism and elitism, and believe that they "shine their own light," they fail to recognize Jesus and their true roles as "priests."

God's gift of free will to us is a powerful tool by which we decide to follow Jesus or not.

Our local bishop and priests attempt to impose their belief of their infallible expertise on God, and that the acts they choose to do and decisions they choose to make with their own free will, no matter how hurtful or harmful, is <u>God's</u> will. They attempt to intimidate and frighten those who question or object to abuses and hurtful actions of the clergy with implications of religious "superiority" and threats of their religious "authority." God would **never** will for His disciples to inflict harm. Simply because actions and decisions are made by "clergy," in **no** way implies that they are God's will. Fortunately God's love and grace <u>always</u> causes good to come of the wrong choices made by humans.

A Jesuit priest once said in his homily, "For one to believe one does not sin is itself a sin of pride."

All humans sin.

So what becomes of sinners?

Who "goes to hell"?

Would the loving God many of us have come to know, ever create a <u>place</u> "hell," of fire, brimstone, and excruciating physical pain? God's infinite love and mercy would never inflict harm. "Hell" <u>is a state of existence we choose ourselves</u>. With God's loving gift of free will, "hell" is where we refuse remorse and reparation; reject God's mercy; and where we ourselves deny our souls from eternal life in God's presence. It is a choice made with our free will <u>to eternally separate ourselves from God</u>. While on earth, human ignorance and arrogance, <u>chooses</u> to ignore or fail to recognize Jesus, and to separate oneself from God.

Some theologians believe that at the end of the world and time, even Satan will convert to God's love and choose to return to be in God's presence; a powerful thought especially to the reality and magnitude of God's love and mercy.

On July 28, 1999, Pope John Paul II during his general audience defined "hell." He said, *"This state of definitive self-exclusion from communion with God and the blessed is called 'hell'"; "a state of those who definitely reject the Father's mercy, even at the last moment of their life."*

There **must,** though, **somewhere** in human vocabularies, in **some** language, **somewhere** in the world, be a term for the state of refusing to recognize God and separating oneself from God in our everyday earthly lives, such as I believe our abusive clergy are doing whenever they believe they are the source of "light," and inflict harm to those they are "called" to serve; or abuse their clerical collar and gift of priesthood.

With lack of easy access to the priest(s) and little visible sense of conscience, remorse, feeling, or accountability, the hurt and harm that priests cause and inflict through their abusive and harmful behavior begins to fester in a place deep inside between the heart and soul of the victim. It festers into an unreconcilable pain, disappointment, and disillusionment not only in the priest(s), but in one's church, friends and family who know that it is not right but stand by and watch it happen, refusing to provide support or take a stand against the wrong, just so as to remain in good favor with the priest because they've been taught to believe that priests can do no wrong and have to be revered no matter what or simply because they are intimidated or afraid to. Relationships amongst friends and families are unfortunately damaged, and even destroyed. It festers to a point where it is impossible to associate around the clergy and to participate at church. This not only hurts that member and family, but the entire Church. Hurt will often fester into anger. One of the sad facts is that the clergy don't understand; one of the saddest facts is that they don't care to understand or to even care at all. In their eyes, everyone is disposable, and there are literally thousands of others who will tell them how wonderful they are, how "holy" they are simply because they have been "ordained" as "priests." We call them "Father," intended for religious and spiritual fatherhood, but it is a title that many priests have no right to assume given the meaning of that word/"title" and the loving examples, which we have each experienced in the personal lives of our parents well lived in love. The title, whenever accepted, comes with the responsibility to care for their "children." Jesus said, *"Call no one on earth your father; you have but one Father in heaven" (Matt. 23:9).* Yet our church institution and its clergy demands the use of that title.

No one can take away our "spiritual" peace…our "shalom";
only **we** can give that away when **we** choose, with our God given
gift of free will, to stop living our faith. But our "religious" peace
within the "organized" religion that we choose to practice our spiritual faith **can** most definitely and absolutely be taken from us. This
occurs **when clergy destroy their credibility as "priests" and cause
division; when we no longer can find peace within the physical
church building(s) and communities we grew up in, lived our lives
around, and love. It is then that we withdraw from our "church."**

"That grave evil" that Pope Francis and theologian Henri De
Lubac referred to, occurs when our church on Main St. USA *"stops
being the 'mysterium lunae," "thinking it has its own light,"* and blinds
us, fails us, betrays, and harms the entire "Church."

The opposite of "hell" is to be in God's presence…the presence
of God's complete "love." Love is part of our lifelong passage, which
begins at the moment we are born. There is a wonderful analogy of
the love in our hearts to a partially full glass of water. The glass of
water is not filled by removing the air and emptiness. The glass is
filled by adding more water. It is said that our hearts are much the
same. We cannot simply remove the emptiness we feel at times or
remove all of the junk, gunk, and hurt. We fill our hearts by adding
more love. Little by little the emptiness is filled and there is no room
left for anything else but more love that "flows" with the "waterfall"
of God's love.

So as "Catholics," what do we say to friends, relatives, or anyone we meet, who tell us they no longer go to church, or that they
are leaving the Catholic Church; or that they have already left the
Catholic Church?

How do we <u>ourselves</u> keep from leaving the Catholic Church after harm inflicted by clergy?

Following the resurrection of Jesus, in the Gospel of Luke the two disillusioned disciples on the road to Emmaus, *were prevented* (not of their choice) *from recognizing Him* (Luke 24:16). In the gospel of John, the disciples fishing in Galilee *"did not realize that it was Jesus."* It is not until after they recognize Jesus, that they were led to powerful encounters with Jesus.

When our priests, **choose** to <u>not</u> live in God's love during their earthly lives and cause harm to others, with little if any sense of remorse, in my opinion, they have chosen to ignore God's presence through their own sense of self-importance, self-interest, and weak faith. They've **chosen** to ignore or to not recognize Jesus.

Each and every one of us knows, where and when we've encountered and experienced God's love. Each and every one of us knows when and where **we've** recognized Jesus! Each and every one of us knows where Jesus has "touched" us and embraced us within His **"Shalom."**

Each of our personal encounters with Jesus, within His shalom, occurs when we recognize and acknowledge His presence and respond, as the *"disciple* [**that**] *Jesus loves."* The unnamed *"disciple Jesus loved"* throughout the gospels of John can only be meant to be each of us. It is **each of us who Jesus loves** who leans against His chest and listens to His heartbeat (John 13:23–25). It is **each of us who Jesus loves** who He sees standing by His cross ready to help and serve others (John 19:26). It is **each of us who Jesus loves** who beholds our Mother Mary and takes and welcomes her into our homes (John 19:27). It is **each of us who Jesus loves** who runs the fastest to Him (outrunning Peter or any priest) because we <u>DO</u> "believe" (John 20:2). It is **each of us who Jesus loves** who recognizes Him, His love and care for us (John 21:4–7). And it is **each of us who Jesus loves** who follows <u>Him</u> until He comes again (John 21:20).

> **When our hearts are ready,**
> **when we're in need of a little help, or**
> **when we simply want to spend some special time with Him,**
> **WE can see and be with JESUS in GALILEE.**

"GALILEE" is a very real place in each of our life journeys.

Galilee

While Jesus was being tortured and crucified, all His disciples were scared and hiding; one even denied knowing Him, for their own self-preservation and self-interest. After the crucifixion of Jesus, on the day of His resurrection, the gospel of Luke describes how two disciples were fleeing Jerusalem, disillusioned and frightened, trying to get away from it all, on their way to Emmaus about seven miles away to the west. On the road and prevented from recognizing Him, they meet up with Jesus. The two invite the stranger, their new best friend to dinner, and the breaking of the bread in their home immediately ignites their encounter with Jesus. Jesus rekindles their hope and the burning in their hearts as the "stranger" on the road spoke to them and opened the scriptures to them, so they immediately return to Jerusalem and meet up with the other disciples, and eventually trek the 120 miles back to GALILEE.

In the account of "The Road to Emmaus," Luke only discloses the name of one of the disciples, Cleopas. Perhaps, and I believe, that the second unnamed disciple on that journey is intended to be each of us; with Jesus opening the scriptures to each and every of us and reminding us of the burning in our hearts which we've experienced during our own individual walks with Jesus in our GALILEE. Where Jesus has blessed us where we've spent our personal and private time with Him have gotten to know Him and know that He is always with us…our "one on one" special and private time with Jesus where we've experienced His "shalom," and have felt blessed, complete, and happy.

According to the gospels of Matthew, many women including Mary Magdalene followed Jesus throughout the agony and crucifixion. After His death and resurrection, they had gone to anoint the body of Jesus which they discovered "missing" from the tomb. They were in panic and distress when they were consoled and reassured by an Angel, and directed to rush and tell the disciples to go to GALILEE where Jesus would meet them. The women rushed off, and on their way, they meet Jesus who greets them and reassures them once again, *"Do not be afraid. Go tell my brothers to go to GALILEE, and there they will see me"* (Matt. 28:10).

In the gospel of John, all the disciples, except for Thomas, were in a house with the doors locked; they were lost, disillusioned, and scared of persecution. Jesus appears and says to them: **Shalom** (*"Peace be with you"*), twice He says **Shalom** (*"peace be with you"*), and for them to *"receive the Holy Spirit"* (John 20:19–22).

One week later, with all the disciples including Thomas locked again in the room, Jesus appears to them and says **Shalom** (*"Peace be with you"*), and questions their faith (John 20:26–29). The disciples then go to GALILEE.

While out on the Sea of GALILEE fishing, Jesus helps them to catch a large load of fish and invites them to have breakfast with Him. He *"took the bread and gave it to them"* (John 21:1–14). At this point, Jesus challenges Peter three times. THREE times he challenges him!: If he loves Him, to "Feed [His] lambs." If he loves Him, to *"Tend* [His] *sheep."* If he loves Him, to *"Feed* [His] *sheep"* (John 21:15–17). This is a crucial and MAJOR command, **repeated THREE**

times, to Peter and the disciples of the Church, that our Catholic clergy way too often **forget**.

Lower **GALILEE** is known to have some of the best climate in that area, with natural springs for water, and rich soil for farming. The Sea of **GALILEE** is the lowest freshwater body of water in the world, which made fishing so prevalent there as is described in the gospels. Mary the mother of Jesus was from Nazareth a village within lower **GALILEE**. Joseph had moved from Jerusalem to **GALILEE** (Nazareth). After fleeing from Herod, from Bethlehem to Egypt, Joseph and Mary walked back with the child Jesus about four hundred miles back to **GALILEE**. Jesus lived His boyhood years in **GALILEE** where they would walk to the Temple in Jerusalem about 120 miles away. When Jesus became a young man, he went from **GALILEE** to Judea and was baptized by John the Baptist in the River Jordan. After the "temptation in the desert" and hearing that John the Baptist had been arrested, Jesus again returned to **GALILEE** and began His ministry and preaching there. Along the banks of the Sea of **GALILEE**, Jesus began the calling of His disciples. For Jesus, and his disciples, **GALILEE** meant a special place! **GALILEE** is where Jesus calls each of us; it is where we each come to know and love Him; it is where he asks us to come see Him and be with Him. **GALILEE** is a special place for each of us to see and be with Jesus.

To most of us "Christians," it would be incredible, and beyond any of our innermost heartfelt imaginings, to experience the charisma and voice of Jesus. "Galileans" were known to have a "dialect" whether or not each of our love for God interprets that as an attribute of "Christians."

The accounts in the gospels of Matthew and Mark describe Peter being rebuked:

> *Surely you too are one of them, even your speech gives you away.* (Matt. 27:73)

> *Surely you are one of them; for you <u>too</u> are a Galilean.* (Mark 15:70)

ALL followers of Jesus have the "**GALILEAN DIALECT**," it is how we are recognized to be carrying God's love through the example of the lives we live each and every day. May we **<u>never</u>** fail to recognize Jesus, deny our roots, lose our "dialect," or betray the love that is nurtured during our times spent with Jesus in each of our "**GALILEE**s."

GALILEE is where the "real" lives of the disciples with Jesus began. It was in **GALILEE** where they spent quality time with Jesus and where they watched many of the miracles performed. They did not understand, though, or appreciate it, until Jesus was crucified and they **thought they had lost <u>everything</u>**. **GALILEE** is the special place where the disciples were directed to return to rediscover what they <u>thought</u> they had lost with the death of Jesus, to rekindle their burning hearts and their discipleships.

When the institution of our Church through our clergy, betrays us (and Jesus), and leaves us reaching out for our "Church," our **"ecclesia catholico,"** we are all called to go to our **GALILEE** where **<u>our</u>** disciple-ships are recharged, inspired, filled, and embraced within His *"shalom."*

<u>Sometimes</u>, priests lovingly inspire us on our journeys; <u>other times,</u> as we witness priests reliving the lives of the Pharisees, high

priests and unholy men, they inflict harm on those they are supposed to serve, deeper than they comprehend, and cast shadows on the ministry of Jesus…on our Church. It is crucial that we learn to recognize when we need to withdraw, to leave our "priests" in their self-glorifying golden temples and take that walk to "GALILEE" where "believing," loving family will join us; where we can each individually be in God's presence and complete love. It is where we can truly gather in a Church such as Jesus intended through His life and ministry, and truly as an *"ecclesia catholico."*

The graces and power of the sacraments come directly from God, not from our priests. Our physical churches are simply buildings where those who want to be "Christians" gather. If any of our "man-made temples" or any portion(s) of our man-made institution of the Catholic Church are destroyed by the hierarchy, clericalism, and abuses of bishops and priests, the "Church of God" continues with Catholic and non-Catholic "Christians" alike, within God's amazing love.

Somewhere throughout our Catholic Church, there ARE authentic priests, who sincerely try to not cast shadows on our churches and who humbly live **only** in the reflection of the light of the Holy Spirit; who humbly and sincerely carry the Bible, the Word of God, above their heads, collars, and mitres, because they understand and know that no one is above the Gospel.

And there are loving, authentic disciples/Christians within our Catholic Church, whether they wear a collar or not, to reach out to, and who will walk with us to our mutual encounter WITH Jesus in our "GALILEE."

When Jesus broke the bread and said *"This is My body, which will be given for you; do this in memory of Me"* (Luke 22:19). They were **not** in a "temple building." They were in a *"guest room"* (Luke 22:11/Mark 14:14) of a large *"upper room"* belonging to a man carrying a *"jar of water"* (symbolic, for only women carried jars of water). "Guest" is defined as to whom hospitality and welcome is extended. When we break bread in our homes and at gatherings with **welcome** and **loved** family and friends, all who are "**present**" in love and "**present**" in prayers of gratitude, Jesus is physically and spiritually available to us. When we are "**present**" in prayer, whether reading a written prayer or simply expressing words and feeling from the heart and with love, Jesus is physically and spiritually available to us. **Wherever** we are, **whoever** we are with, **whatever** we are doing, if we are savoring the moment and praying "Thank you, God!" in humbleness, Jesus is physically and spiritually available to us.

God calls us to be His mouth, hands, and feet. **Whatever we do in and with "love" is "good."** Whenever we are living in "love," we are in God's church; we are in "**GALILEE.**"

We each know when we recognize Jesus and feel God's presence in a very physical and special way; we each recognize that encounter. "**GALILEE**" is a very real and physical place on our "passage." The "**GALILEE**" where we are <u>invited</u> and <u>welcomed</u> by Jesus truly does exist!

Each and every one of us is called by God to **choose** "love"; to **speak** with His "love dialect," and to **meet** Him and **be with** Him, in "**GALILEE.**"

THAT is the "Church" of **Jesus**. **THAT** is the "Church" filled with the **Holy Spirit**.

THAT is **GOD's** "**CHURCH.**"

"Collars" are **not** required.

"Come meet Me in Galilee."

Closing Prayers and Anticipation

*[SHALOM!] "Do not be afraid. Go tell my brothers to go to **GALILEE**, and there they will see Me"* (Matt. 28:10).

[and be with Me]

God bless us <u>all</u>.

In the name of the Father, and of the Son, and of the Holy Spirit.

Amen.

Heavenly Father,

Help us when we or anyone we love has been
mistreated, ignored, abused, or harmed

in any form or magnitude

by a member or members of our clergy and their clerical abuses

and/or hurt by other members of our Church family.

Help us to never turn <u>our</u> backs on those who are hurt.

Help us to always be loving

kind, unselfish, and compassionate to others;

to keep our hearts wide open to You

to trust in Your love and continue Your mission

Even when it makes us vulnerable to being
hurt or at great personal cost.

Help us to remain focused on You

and to Your love

Help us to always remember the way to our "GALILEE."

Amen.

*I look forward to meeting and seeing you in **GALILEE**!*

*I pray never having to withdraw to the point of
abandoning our "Catholic" "Church."*

*But whether we do or not, and regardless of the example of our
Catholic clergy and <u>institution</u> of our Church, may we be **"relentless"**
with **"parresia,"** to the teachings and love of Jesus Christ.*

We are all worthy of God's love.

*We all deserve a welcome, loving "place" to truly
"gather" in God's name and in His love.*

*We may not see the transformation of our Catholic Church
in our lifetimes, but we may see the transformation
of our lives to who God created us to be.*

God bless us and hold us in the warmth of His embrace.

Shalom!

About the Author

Rick Anthony Cordova is a professional engineer by trade in private practice. Growing up, Rick attended a private Catholic grade school (part of the cathedral) where he and his brothers were dedicated altar servers prior to continuing on to Catholic high school. Rick is a lifelong Catholic of generational family and friends at the beautiful historic cathedral of his diocese. Engineering analyticity, religion, and spirituality go hand in hand, which enforces a deeper understanding, and also a struggle with our Church's two thousand years of status quo.

CPSIA information can be obtained
at www.ICGtesting.com
Printed in the USA
BVHW091236230323
661006BV00021B/1002